D0041776

INNOVATIVE
COLLEGE
MANAGEMENT

Implementing Proven
Organizational Practice

Robert E. Lahti

INNOVATIVE
COLLEGE
MANAGEMENT

 Jossey-Bass Publishers
San Francisco • Washington • London • 1973

LB
2341
.L23

INNOVATIVE COLLEGE MANAGEMENT
Implementing Proven Organizational Practice
by Robert E. Lahti

Copyright © 1973 by: Jossey-Bass, Inc., Publishers
615 Montgomery Street
San Francisco, California 94111

&

Jossey-Bass Limited
3 Henrietta Street
London WC2E 8LU

Copyright under International, Pan American, and
Universal Copyright Conventions. All rights
reserved. No part of this book may be reproduced
in any form—except for brief quotation (not to
exceed 1,000 words) in a review or professional
work—without permission in writing from the publishers.

Library of Congress Catalogue Card Number LC 73-10938

International Standard Book Number ISBN 0-87589-191-8

Manufactured in the United States of America

JACKET DESIGN BY WILLI BAUM

FIRST EDITION

Code 7333

The Jossey-Bass
Series in Higher Education

JOHN E. ROUECHE, *University of Texas*

Special Advisor, Community and Junior Colleges

55908

Preface

A wide gap exists between available professional managerial knowledge and its application in the collegiate setting. The explosion of experience, research, and study primarily in business and industry is potentially useful for all organizations, including nonprofit educational institutions. Some educators, however, are unwilling to replace entrenched managerial traditions and are reluctant to launch new systems for management. There is little that is more difficult, more open to criticism, or more perilous to execute than the initiation of a new order of operation.

Can managerial knowledge used by profit organizations be effectively applied to nonprofit organizations? I believe that it can. Obviously, distinct operational differences exist, but much managerial knowledge has broad application to all organizations regardless of their character. Some organizations are small and struggling to exist; others are large and sliding along on past successes. Some are oriented to manufacturing products for profit; others offer nonprofit services. But all have one factor in common: they involve people, through whom work is effectively or ineffectively accomplished.

The principles of successful management are no less important to education than they are to industry. Planning, goal setting, and coping with change are just as necessary to a college as they are to a profit-oriented business. The need to motivate, reward, and develop people is not the exclusive need of profit organizations.

Fortunately, some management concepts used successfully by profit organizations are slowly beginning to filter into the nonprofit structure. Perhaps profit-oriented management could be actively helpful in the transfer of useable knowledge to the nonprofit organizations that are a vital part of our society. To improve their efficiency is in everyone's best interest.

Innovative College Management aims to narrow the gap between what can be done and what is being done to bring about efficient management of educational institutions. In themselves, the presentations here are not to be construed as the sole answers to problems besetting many collegiate institutions today. They are proposed approaches, primarily borrowed from profit organizations and translated for application in the nonprofit higher education setting. Initiation of these approaches, and perhaps even more daring innovation, will, I hope, help restore public confidence in the institutions of higher education. Fundamental to the approaches offered herein is the assumption that educators in managerial roles must recognize the need for, and accept an aggressive and creative role in, identifying and correcting trouble spots.

Aimed at the practicing educational manager and those aspiring to management, *Innovative College Management* seeks to help managers steeped in theory but unable to execute essential programs successfully. Although educational institutions are the training ground for most educational managers, their inability to apply their teaching to their organizations

Preface

is not only ironic but increases public intolerance. This book provides the educational manager with some insight into what educational management is about in practice; it serves as a guide to help him objectively assess his own work, diagnose his weaknesses, and take measures for effective performance.

Although *Innovative College Management* focuses primarily on the two-year college, many of the same approaches and principles could beneficially be applied to all educational institutions. Major emphasis is on managing through a logical and measurable objectives approach. The importance of the human dimension and the necessity for insight into human behavior to guarantee quality performance are essential underpinnings. This managerial frontier perhaps deserves time and space of its own to fully explore means of utilizing human abilities and energies effectively for constructive results.

I gratefully acknowledge the help of those individuals who assisted either directly or indirectly with this book. A special thanks to my dear wife, Ruth, who encouraged and assisted me through many months and to Renee, Randy, and Ryan who were such understanding children during the whole project. If this publication contributes to or in any way inspires a continued attempt to innovate and to increase the effectiveness of college management, it will have accomplished my purpose.

Palatine, Illinois   ROBERT E. LAHTI
September 1973

Contents

Contents

INNOVATIVE
COLLEGE
MANAGEMENT

Implementing Proven
Organizational Practice

Chapter 1

Management of Change

Recent social and economic changes have created new urgencies in national priorities. Environmental control, the population explosion, public health and welfare, and poverty are among the issues competing for the financial and intellectual resources of the nation. Yet just when higher education should be most competently contributing to the fulfillment of priority demands, our colleges are laboring under a confidence crisis.

They are suffering the inward turmoil of hostile and confused constituencies and a resulting "bad press" which has led to a public questioning of their capability for self-goverance.

In November 1972 a Harris Survey pinpointed a decline of confidence in the leadership of American institutions. In 1966, 61 percent of the people expressed "a great deal of confidence" in educational leadership; in 1972 this figure had dropped to 33 percent. These figures reemphasize an educator's priority: to better assess the need for change in educational programs.

Innovative College Management

Internally, institutions are frequently weakened by inefficient management and decision-making and resulting inefficiencies in utilization of facilities and monetary resources. Many have not been able to establish their own priorities, much less national priorities. Problems in higher education now can be attributed to yesterday's failures in planning, lack of foresight, cultural changes, and the management requirements of today's complex institutions.

There are disturbing—even crucial—indications that institutions are not fully serving educational needs and are losing their sense of purpose. The inability of colleges to cope with modern change has many an administrator feeling like a man who tries to drive a horse-drawn carriage on an expressway: He lacks the skill, the vehicle, and sometimes the courage to keep pace with the traffic or even to control his own direction. Critics suggest that today's collegiate institution must scrap or at least retread the traditional organizational vehicle if it is to cope with change.

Diagnosing the ills of colleges and universities has become a popular pursuit of writers, politicians, businessmen, and academicians. Although the critics may differ in specifics, there is a central theme dominant in all: that collegiate systems of governance are under fire and need reform.

McFeely (1972, p. 1) states, "There are times in the history of every institution when what seems needed is a major overhaul—a marked change in the strategic structure of the organization . . ." Lessinger (1971)` comments, "It is strange that we are passive about demanding performance of our schools . . . But our schools keep rolling along doing the same old thing in the same old way. Even if we demanded better performance, our schools would be unable to deliver . . ."

The president of the Academy for Educational Development, Inc. (Eurich, 1970, pp. 18–22) believes the key to survival is good planning—specifically long-range planning,

2

which means setting manageable goals. He lists the critical problems facing colleges and universities today to be vague, poorly defined objectives; outmoded and inefficient teaching techniques; lack of top quality teachers and administrators; disagreement about top priorities; and inefficient use of facilities. He goes on to say that "planning is tried and proven in business; in education, it is still an exciting frontier. But this lag suggests that we must turn to the task with alacrity. Time is short for getting higher education's house in order . . ."

Further confirmation of the need for reform is offered by an authority on management (Odiorne, 1972) who comments, "Once you know where you want to go, organization charts and planning become means for getting there . . . Get your objectives clear and organize in the way that is most likely to help you achieve them. If, in the process, you have to throw out some old organizational theories, don't worry. If they won't work, they weren't very good to begin with."

Management consultant Keane (1970) warns, "There will be increasing pressure on the nation's colleges and universities to make more effective use of available resources through improved management and administrative techniques. . . . The most serious management problem of most colleges and universities is that they do not have clearly defined goals. . . . If an institution does not have a very clear idea of its roles and goals, it obviously has no basis for determining whether it is effectively organized or managed."

Perhaps the greatest stress has come to bear on the elite institutions, some liberal arts colleges, and the private colleges. The public community colleges fare somewhat better; they had little if any student dissent, operation costs are relatively low, they have closer communication with those they serve, and they are newer. But though they are being recognized as a unique addition to postsecondary education, they are not immune to the problems facing higher education in general.

3

They suffer from the same lack of effective management and must recognize and deal with the same specific problems and needs.

Proper Executive Orientation. Many community college presidents do not understand or perhaps do not wish to accept the full responsibility of a chief executive officer of a multimillion dollar institution. This shortcoming is not surprising in view of the rapidity with which some such presidents arrive at their posts, the quality of training—if any—they receive, and the unsophisticated manner in which college presidents are chosen. When an individual accepts the chief executive officer's role, he assumes responsibility for planning, organization, and governance. As the institutional leader he is primarily accountable for student learning; he is the institution's representative and spokesman and must maintain relationships with the board as well as with local, state, and federal agencies. As an effective manager, he will plan for management succession and establish training and development programs for his assistants.

Drucker (quoted in Goble, p. 1) put it rather succinctly: "If an enterprise fails to perform, we rightly hire not different workers but a new president." However, most leaders would maintain that this principle is less applicable today because of the gradual erosion of the authority of the president, the advent of collective bargaining in higher education, the increased sensitivity to academic freedom, the increased emphasis on participative decision-making, and faculty involvement in governance.

Board Performance and Compensation. The importance of leadership and of support for effective leadership is obvious. The casual way in which many college trustees select and reward executives in highly pressured jobs and their failure to provide development and rehabilitation for those individuals are partially responsible for the ineffectiveness of some such administrators. An ideal board is composed of individuals who represent a variety of disciplines and can therefore contribute useful knowledge to the organization. Self-perpetuating boards gradually lose the energy and creativity necessary to stimulate and maintain their contribution to a management team. Effectiveness is closely related to the competence of the board chairman. He or she must have a good general knowledge of the organization, as must the president, yet must not attempt to act as an administrator. Because the board chooses the president, it determines the success or failure of the organization.

Once the board has selected the chief executive officer, it should be prepared to offer a comprehensive administrative and faculty compensation program. The manager must clarify administrative goals and then establish a positive motivational plan. The rewards should be commensurate with responsibility, risks, and results. The institution must still be given top priority, however, and the plan should provide the most compensation at the smallest expense to the organization.

With motivation, the board will yield greater results for the organization and will achieve a commendable standard of performance, too often lacking in the two-year college. The board should prepare a written statement of broad corporate policy, establish long- and short-term objectives, and develop a long term plan for meeting those objectives. The job of the chief executive officer is defined, and a standard of performance for him is approved. When he is appointed, he is given the confidence and support of the board through assistance and counsel. Duties and responsibilities of the chairman and members of the board are defined, and provision is made for constructive board meetings.

Definition of Managerial Authority. In community college management as in management of four-year colleges, authority is poorly defined. Historically, the authority of the boards in two-year colleges has been limited by traditional

5

high school practices, and in some cases these practices are set by law. One of the greatest management needs of the rapidly expanding, diverse community college is a much clearer definition of management authority and establishment of an identifiable management structure that will make the institution more accountable for its effectiveness.

The increasing consensus among experts is that an organization has its greatest chance of achieving maximum effectiveness when it seriously concerns itself with priorities, goals, and effective evaluative techniques. The organization must provide a hospitable environment for its workers where goals replace conformity, competence replaces authority, renewal opportunities prevail, and a system for rewarding individual performance is practiced.

Organization. One of the more controversial aspects of leadership in business, industry, and government as well as in education is the creation of the most effective organization. Several distinguished behavioral scientists have suggested that the simpler the structure in organization, the better. (As part of a study by the Conference Board, a nonprofit business research organization (Rush, 1970, pp. 9–10), on the influence of behavioral scientists, their work, and their theories, seven stood out as ones businessmen seemed most interested in: Douglas McGregor, Frederick Herzberg, Rensis Likert, Chris Argyris, Abraham Maslow, Robert Blake and Jane S. Mouton.) It is popular in academic circles to imply that too much organization inhibits growth, creativity, and flexibility and often results in an authoritarian style of leadership. At the other extreme are countless organizations that have failed through too little rather than too much structure. The community college must develop its organizational policy to incorporate workable solutions to its specific obvious problems.

Community college educators have been accused of

trying to be all things to all people; these educators must establish priorities that demonstrate to the public the effectiveness of their community-oriented institutions.

Community college educators must put into practice behavioral scientists' proven methods of initiating and building dynamic organizations. The community college leader must understand organizational dynamics and the demands of people versus those of the organization.

The administrator must be sensitive to appropriate or inappropriate leadership styles in motivating workers. Awareness of his own leadership style and how to use it effectively will enhance the potential of the organization to reach its goals.

As with any effective organization, a community college must arrange priorities and set specific goals against which to develop measures of success. In the past, the broad goals of community colleges and other higher educational institutions have lacked operational meaning and definitive measurement.

The contemporary community college administrator must know and practice the functions of an effective manager and be able to carry them out with confidence and success. He must fully assume the responsibility and accountability for the health and environmental climate of his organization, its structure, and the effectiveness of its operational processes.

It is of utmost importance that the managerial functions within the participative environmental structure be well identified: in other words, who does what; who is responsible for what; and what are the divided responsibilities of the board of trustees, the management, the teaching faculty, the supportive staff, and the students.

Community college administrators must understand and influence the use of appropriate experimental design, methods of research, and evaluation techniques. Through competence and understanding, leadership should assume the responsibility for providing the resources and wherewithal to upgrade the teaching faculty in research and evaluation processes.

The community college has been classified as the truly American contribution to higher education and considers itself to be the innovative addition to the higher education movement; therefore, community college educators must understand the characteristics of a creative organization and know how to reinforce creativity among its constituent individuals.

Community college administrators must be willing to accept and utilize proven management tools and techniques in the operation of their organizations, acknowledging that these management tools and systems may need interpretation and delicate application to higher education. It is imperative that the two-year college examine such management tools as MBO, PPBS, PERT, performance evaluation techniques, and proven cost effectiveness measures.

Managerial leadership must accept and practice by example the reductive use of authority through competence, through control of process by goals, and through reward systems for reinforcing individual performance.

The community college manager must better understand the traditional role and function of the board of trustees, including the legalistic role established by each state. Additionally, the chief executive officer must offer leadership and counsel and exemplify confidence to the board of trustees as well as to all other organizational constituencies. If they are not spelled out by law, the chief executive officer must operationalize guidelines and job responsibilities for the board of trustees in contrast to his own. It is becoming more and more important in a time of accountability that the chief executive officer and his board of trustees agree upon effective measures of evaluating each other's performance.

8

Management of Change

The community college manager must be prepared to face conflict resolution; he must solve problems effectively with a minimum of rationalizing.

It is becoming increasingly more important that chief executive officers and their trustees acknowledge the importance of identifying and staffing the personnel functions of the college effectively. These functions should include resources for the establishment and operation of a well-rounded personnel program including special competence in labor relations, collective bargaining, wage and salary administration, and affirmative action programs.

Because of the uniqueness of the community college and its inability to recruit knowledgeable administrators, it is becoming more apparent that developmental programs need to be initiated at least for administrators and faculty. In the case of the community college manager, the development of his staff is a function for which he should be held accountable and is the responsibility of each employee in this newly evolving institution.

Because of the continued expected growth of community colleges and the necessity for continuity in management within each college, a progressive community college executive must have in mind a managerial succession plan resulting from the management development program.

Because of the recent frequency of law suits arising from non-retention, suspension, and firing, it will become necessary for community college managers to formalize and sophisticate their recruitment and selection processes and to guarantee due process procedures for all personnel.

Because of the diversity of programs and, in some cases, their short-lived needs, it will become increasingly important that community college administrators establish a process for eliminating ineffective programs or those that cannot justify their cost of operation. Renewed public confidence will be

9

created when administrators are able to introduce more programs or techniques that reduce costs or promote greater efficiency.

Community college administrators must place increasing emphasis on the evaluation of job performance on a more objective basis; past indifference to or difficulty in assessing job performance and the concomitant commitment to the welfare of the individual has contributed to lesser productivity and probably a higher cost of operation.

Community college administrators and faculty must consider increased human productivity as great a resource for solving financial problems as additional local taxes, student tuition, state income, or federal support.

Administrators and faculty must accept and be strong proponents of the community college concept rather than measuring success in terms of academic degrees. At the same time, community college administrators and faculty must acknowledge the goal of baccalaureate and graduate education as one of the preparatory missions of a community college.

The community college administrator must recognize the distinction between long-range planning and institutional research and recognize institutional research as first priority. Institutional research collects, analyzes, interprets, and reports information, whereas planning focuses upon goals, purposes, committee work, methods for achieving goals, and quantitative decisions. With accelerated changes occurring in revised academic calendars, interdisciplinary studies, experiential learning, and new technologies, additional institutional research is needed so that educational planners keep their focus on the moving target. A further dilemma for two-year college administrators is the extent to which institutional research should be administratively or educationally organized. Both emphases are essential. Although they can be separated intellectually they cannot be considered independent operationally and must

10

be coordinated and unified. Administrative research and educational research must interface.

The relevance and cost justification of the computer on a sizeable community college campus may not be validated until the planning process on campus has matured to a point where administrators and faculties are aware of the need to simulate, choose alternatives, and implement computer assisted instruction on a cost effectiveness basis. Additionally, it will take a sizeable campus with ample resources to implement the cost of a developmental staff for creating software packages for the entire organization as opposed to the hiring of a core operational staff who might involve themselves in moderate software package building or modifying packages that are already on the market. Of course, the institution that chooses to modify software packages might suffer from loss of "pride of authorship" or lack of programs perfectly designed to meet their needs. College management will perhaps feel better when comparing the cost of a full developmental staff with that of a smaller core operational staff. The community college president must take a hard look at the cost of computer hardware he has on campus, the cost benefits accruing to the organization, and the status of possessing its own computer.

The fundamental building block of all organizations is people. Is it unreasonable to believe that motivation techniques that work essentially well in one organization should have no significance in another? Can anyone who is familiar with planning and goal setting doubt that these techniques can add effectiveness to any organization? Is creativity something that business needs but colleges disregard? Is there any reason to believe that the problems of communication in business and industry are radically different from those in other organizations? Is the selection of the right person for the right task only important in the business and industrial world? Is research, especially procedural or operational research, something that nonprofit organizations should indulge in to a greater extent? Is there any reason to believe that leadership is the difference between success and failure in business but is less important for the two-year college?

Proven management techniques and systems cannot be ignored by educational managers. Although implementation in and application to the educational setting may require translation and modification, these techniques may well demonstrate new approaches to old problems; they are intended not as an assault on the approaches used in the past but rather as means of meeting the obvious evidence that old methods are no longer effective.

This book offers insight to better and modern management of the two-year college and to the process of developing more competent managers. The publication focuses on the utilization of a management system known as Management by Objectives and other proven management processes and techniques that extend or are compatible with the MBO system.

Chapter 2

Establishing a Basis for Effective Management

Cognizance of the problems is only the beginning in assessing where we are, where we are going, and how we are going to get there. Where we are going is determined in large part by goals and objectives established. If there are none, the answer is obvious.

Goal setting is next to meaningless if it is too vague and does not spell out why to do it, how much of it to do, and what things we have to do it with. In other words, appropriate goals must be realistic and sensible so that the outcome is worthwhile.

Higher education decision makers often go to great lengths to find out what programs cost but make decisions and formulate plans with little or no idea of what the outcome will be. All too often goals become merely wishful thinking, sterile ideas confined to writing, or a planning process of some fashion to be gotten through and then abandoned. What is needed is an understanding of the crucial relationships of goals on the one hand, desired outcome on the other, and the various activities necessary to move from one to the other so that making judgments about goals and assessing activities and resources will be translated into results.

There are six specific management problems that must be dealt with in achieving organizational effectiveness.

The first is how to integrate individual needs and organizational goals. Although organizations are formed by men and composed of men to fulfill the objectives of men, a competition exists between the satisfaction of individual needs and the fulfillment of organizational goals. As noted by Chris Argyris, a behavioral scientist, the traditional organization not only fails to recognize the higher level needs of the individual but thwarts them. The effectiveness of the organization and the individual are blocked.

The second consideration is power and how power is distributed. The traditional, bureaucratic pyramid of power is no longer effective in a climate of technological and educational diversification. Power distribution must move from a completely autocratic to a more democratic basis for the greater utilization of vital human resources. The one-man rule which prevails in management, for example, becomes obsolete when one man can no longer possess all the knowledge required for the decisions that must be made by an organization.

Thirdly, managing and resolving conflicts must be considered. As organizations become more complex, they fragment and divide. They become composed of inner groups that often work to exclude others and on some occasions to exploit differences.

Adapting to a turbulent environment is the fourth problem. The organizational environment, both internal and external, is rapidly changing. Any organization that is to survive must mold itself according to constantly changing environmental elements. For example, higher educational institutions are increasingly enmeshed in legislation and public policy. The government is, and will become, more and more involved. The managerial molding of the college or university must strive for organizational adaptation required by this involvement.

The fifth problem is one of identity. Because rapid growth and turbulence can distort original goals, community colleges are extremely vulnerable to identity crises. As changing conditions require constant amendment of goals, the clarification of identity becomes a continuous problem. For example, a university that was organized to transmit knowledge to students often finds that it is now as much involved in research for government as it is in teaching.

The sixth problem is growth and decay. Revitalization to avoid decay depends upon the ability to learn from experience, to develop methods for improving the learning process, to be self-analytical, and to direct one's own destiny. Such revitalization must be a continuous process within the organization.

Effective management requires a knowledge of human behavior to build organizations in which the constituents are led to perform for the organization at the highest possible level of their potential. This goal may require the development of a more creative internal climate within the human being (his attitudes, abilities, knowledge) and a more creative climate provided by his environment. Mounting interest in human values, problems in traditional management modes that treat employees as tools, measures sought to enhance man as an innovator, all point to the recognition that the process of creativity plays a major role in successful management techniques.

A creative environment is the basis of a dynamic organization, achieves its continually renewed objectives, is structured to cope with new ideas and to utilize change in its advancement, and functions by the cohesiveness of its working forces. Such an organization is recognized by its competitors, colleagues, and the public it serves, and recognizes itself as a pacesetter in its field. It attracts the highest caliber personnel, advances the development of its personnel, and instills confidence within its employees and in the public it serves.

The creative organization may be best described as one that maintains an atmosphere of involvement, one that encourages employees to become fully participative. An environment should exist that encourages society or groups of peers rather than a rigid hierarchy; there should be a relative lack of social distance between the employees and their supervisors at every echelon of management. Because the individual is the organization's most important resource, major focus should be placed on providing him with the things he needs to enable him to work at his best. Work should be challenging, interesting, and personally rewarding, and assignments, responsibility, and authority should be delegated with this aim in mind. A great deal of trust should be placed in each person; there should be a minimum of controls, constraints, and external forces telling him how to do his job, and formal policies, procedures, and standards should provide a platform from which he can operate rather than a set of inflexible rules confining him. Great emphasis should be placed on quality and technical excellence, and long-term career opportunities and personal growth potential should be available. Emphasis should be placed on internal upward mobility and on offering individuals diversified job assignments. The employee should be given opportunities for achieving his maximum capabilities rather than be pigeonholed in a position where he has already proved himself. Stress should be placed on delegation of

authority and responsibility downward through the organization; persons who will be directly affected by management decisions should be given the opportunity to participate in the decision-making process.

The truly successful organization maintains this climate of involvement. The involvement of people in planning and in governing their work does not come instantaneously, however. Time, effort, and development are required if this concept is to be meaningful, and competency in leadership is a key factor.

Leadership aspirants must know how to exercise their authority in a way that is appropriate to the characteristics of the situation and to the people involved. Above all, they need to learn that the real source of their power is their own knowledge and skill and the strength of their own personalities, not the authority conferred upon them by their positions.

Managing the rapid change in technology and utilizing behavioral science research to elicit maximum human effort are two great challenges of organizational leadership today. Over all it seeks to make each employee responsible not only for doing his job better but also for participating in planning, controlling, and appraising the outcome. Effective leaders must lead through competency, which breeds respect, and not through force, which breeds fear. The competent leader brings to his position the strength of his ability; for this he is respected and gains the support and willingness of his followers. Hitler is a classic example of authoritative leadership—a man at the right place at the right time assuming a leadership role regardless of competence. History has dramatically shown that authoritative leadership (leadership by force) can result in rebellion, lack of productivity, and intolerance. Many approaches and research studies have concerned themselves with the study of leadership; it may be summed up as the ability to get the appropriate things done through people in order that predetermined objectives be met. Therefore, leadership em-

17

bodies versatile, flexible roles that are responsive to the demands of the particular situation. The leader must be capable of assessing which conditions promote and which thwart the best talent of his people. By objectively sizing himself up he is able to assess which of a variety of leadership roles may best serve a particular situation.

Effective leadership maintains a control stemming from commitment by the employees to set and reach realistic objectives. Leading in the traditional sense perhaps means planning what the job is; imposing rules, regulations, and training to accomplish it; and overseeing control and discipline to assure the desired outcome. Creative goal-oriented leadership may embody many of the same processes but emphasizes the participation and motivation of people by involving them in the processes of planning, controlling, appraising, and conflict resolution. This leadership provides an environment wherein the employees feel they are working for themselves. Leadership, if goal-oriented, usually does not attempt to hinder the employee's management of his own work by unnecessarily overseeing him or possibly getting in the way. This does not mean that leadership abdicates responsibility for getting the job done well; rather, if leadership is strong in the beginning stages or at the time of participative planning, those processes that follow require less direct supervision.

A leader must know himself, be able to see himself as others see him, and be genuinely sensitive to how he affects other people. He understands and is sensitive to the motivational needs of his followers and takes pride in their accomplishments knowing that their achievements and growth, if recognized and commended, will only produce greater motivation and productivity.

The leader must give visibility to organizational objectives, provide necessary resources, mediate conflict, solve problems, and provide a climate where people feel they are

managing their own work. Subordinates will seek counsel from an effective supervisor if he has earned their respect and has knowledge and competence that will assist in the achievement of their goals.

Essentially, true leaders are able to assess themselves accurately and to do what is necessary within their limitations to get the right things done. There are important characteristics, however, that contribute to excellence in leadership and can be valuable to managers at all levels. Ambition—the desire or drive to achieve—suggests courage to forge ahead, which can enable the leader to become a catalyst for getting things started. With persistence even under pressure or in face of failure or insurmountable obstacles, the effective leader can push forward. Confidence includes the capability of making definite and unwavering decisions. It includes self-control and an inward assurance of being able to successfully direct others. A sense of honesty, integrity, and sincerity in dealing with others demands honesty in return, and without it the leader cannot command the respect of his followers. Also important is a sense of justice—an equitable and fair approach to any matter. As with honesty, justice practiced can better command justice in return. With objectivity, the ability to perceive things as they really are, excellent leaders are able to face reality and to detect that which is false, pretentious, or dishonest. The flexibility to shift gears as the situation dictates is necessary. Inflexibility locks the leader into a set pattern of thinking or behavior and thereby stifles his effectiveness in coping with people, problems, and leadership in general.

Numerous other qualifications attributable to leadership excellence warrant mentioning: creativity, pleasing personality, sympathy, understanding, cooperation, emotional maturity, and certainly a charismatic leadership style.

If leadership is to remain vibrant and dynamically effective, it must have avenues of revitalization or ways to renew its energies, to maintain a relevancy between the organization it leads and the external environment, and to enhance creative and imaginative new approaches. Leadership that is allowed or forced to become placid soon breeds placidity in its followers, and laxity or poor productivity begins to permeate the whole organization. Pressures, unpredictable schedules, and hard demands for ever-increasing efficiency can erode clarity of thought, objectivity, and enthusiasm for the job if periodic intervals are not made available for self-renewal and professional growth. Like other management levels, the top level of management needs additional stimulation to maintain a high degree of energy, motivation, productivity, and excellence.

Chapter 3

Performance Standards for Trustee Effectiveness

The relationship of the president of an organization and the board of trustees must be an increasingly creative force to improve institutional effectiveness in accordance with the changing needs of the organization's service area. To accomplish this goal requires the chief executive and the board of trustees to answer such questions as: How are sound working relationships established? What are the respective roles of the board and its chief executive? What is the collective role of board members operating as a policy-making body? To what extent should trustees be involved with internal details of the institution? What is a well-balanced board? What are the desirable qualifications for a board member? How do trustees coordinate their activities as a unit? What is the nature of each board office? And, particularly, what is the special nature of the board chairman's role?

A frequent obstacle to managerial effectiveness is a

board whose members neither understand what institutional management is nor comprehend their role in it. To increase such understanding is the challenge and responsibility of the chairman of the board and the chief executive officer. The president of an institution and some of his top executives are frequently called upon to offer advice and counsel to individual board members. Advice offered from a lack of understanding of board-administrative relationships or insufficient background on the proper role of a trustee may lead to misunderstandings and a confusion of roles. Additionally, understanding trustee-ship is important to top administrators since they are frequently called upon to serve as trustees for various community organizations.

It is important, therefore, that the president and his top managers be able to communicate proven concepts of trustee-ship that make a board effective and to clearly outline the functions and authority of trustees; to identify areas of responsibilities and control for the board; to show the direct relationship of productive management to the successful functioning of the board and to the rapport that must exist between a board of trustees and top management personnel, particularly the chief executive.

Trustee effectiveness, a problem that concerns both private and public institutions, is rarely, if ever, mentioned by an administrator directly to his board. Yet it must be faced, discussed, and resolved if the institution is to remain vibrant and is to serve the changing needs of its constituencies.

Boards of trustees have an extremely significant role in the scheme of effective management, and they should recognize the nature and importance of the positions in which they have been legally placed. Their effectiveness depends not simply on the decisions they are required to make and how or when they

22

make them but on how well they understand and then perform their responsibilities.

Administrators cannot achieve organizational changes or guarantee organizational effectiveness alone; they need the guidance and support of competent trustees. The dilemma of an established institution's serving a changing public has been dramatically described by John Gardner, public interest lobbyist and former Secretary of Health, Education, and Welfare. Gardner describes the creative tension that arises between the public's demand for change in a society of rising expectations and the lack of flexibility of institutions—public and private—in reflecting these mandates and pressures. The vitality and future of educational institutions, according to Gardner, depends wholly upon the affection, concern, and criticism of those charged with their future.

Educational renewal, change, and, indeed, survival depend on persons who combine compassionate concern with careful criticism of the institutions that serve them. Educational institutions and those who direct them need to be aware of the fine distinction between being critical lovers and loving critics.

Board members of two-year colleges are commonly called trustees because they are involved in trust relationships. The trust responsibilities include managing the institution in the public interest; being accountable to official bodies and to the public for actions taken and funds used; carrying out responsibilities involved in the education of students; and holding title to, administering, and executing other trusts. A board of trustees is generally accountable for receiving and disbursing funds, authorizing the budget, holding properties, appointing the president, entering into contracts, formulating long-range plans, and exercising final authority on other matters relating to the management and control of the organization as stated by law. It faces immensely complex educational decisions involving the common management triangle of man, money, and change. It must also deal with the teaching staff, administrator-board relationships, and broadened community responsibilities in attempting to develop the institution as a comprehensive community college.

As the complexity of organizations increases and the trust relationship is magnified by size, a most important consideration for continuity in organizational effectiveness is the qualifications of board members. Although the public sector's method of selection through political appointment or election does not always yield qualified board members, citizens, chief administrators, and fellow board members should still try to maintain a well-balanced board.

Qualities considered important for effective board members are honesty and integrity; ability to contribute to board balance; success in a field of endeavor; meaningful business experience; managerial capabilities; stature in the community; maturity; knowledge of, or willingness to become a student of, organizational dynamics; dedicated interest in the organization; willingness to devote time to the job; objectivity; lack of political or personal motivation; ability to work harmoniously with other members; absence of conflicting interests; ability to advise and appraise management; ability to make a contribution to the organization; and a sincere desire to offer a civic service with either little or no remuneration. Although one might suggest that such a board member has not been born yet, one can hardly question the validity of these qualities in terms of their potential for enhancing board effectiveness.

The importance of board qualifications is again underscored when one reviews basic but specifically significant responsibilities which are common to a variety of boards. These include the safeguarding and husbanding of the organization's

24

total assets (financial, physical, and human) in the interests of the consumer and the taxpayer; determination of goals and objectives after appropriate staff involvement; selection of the chief executive officer and key subordinates; provision of organizational stability; approval of long-range plans; critique and validation of results; and approval of compensation practices.

There are educational institutions whose total boards are ineffective or include at least some ineffective trustees. If performed improperly, the board's role can affect the quality of the instructional program, the performance of the management personnel, and the morale of staff and students. When the chairman of the board is approached on the subject of an ineffective trustee or an ineffective board, decisions or evaluations are generally not forthcoming because there are no precedents. Few rules or regulations cover this predicament. Moreover, a weak trustee may be an important and influential individual or a personal friend of the college president or the chairman of the board, and therefore the problem may be swept under the rug. The effective administrator must recognize the problem and take initiative in resolving it. The most obvious indications that a trustee is ineffective are poor or irregular attendance at board meetings, advanced age, poor health, and failure to do homework prior to meeting time. Ineffective performances may also be due to inadequate information from management, inadequate orientation to the institution and to trusteeship, lack of specifically assigned duties or responsibilities, or too long a term as trustee.

The solution lies in the development of standards of performance for board effectiveness. Specific performance objectives enhance the effectiveness of the board of trustees as well as that of the individual trustee. These standards are expressed in a well-written statement of the conditions that should prevail when a job has been properly accomplished (see implementation section, p. 152). The standards must encompass those elements that make an organization effective: a serious concern for effective planning; well-defined priorities and goals; effective evaluation techniques; and a hospitable environment for workers in which goals replace conformity, competence replaces authority, renewal opportunities prevail, and individual excellence is rewarded.

Specific performance standards begin with a well-written statement of the purpose for which the organization exists. This statement enables the board to develop a written definition of its powers as well as its duties and responsibilities as interpreted from state statute. The board must represent the institution to the public and the public to the institution and, in both cases, serve as a buffer for the institution. The primary power and responsibility of the board is to conduct, manage, and control the affairs of the college by means of policies consistent with the law. With these purposes in mind, the board must establish long- and short-range objectives for the college as well as a long-range plan for meeting those objectives.

Job definitions that delineate duties, responsibilities, objectives, and performance schedules should be drawn up for the president, the chairman of the board, individual trustees, board committees, and task forces. The standard of performance for the president should be agreed upon by both the board and the president. Essential for the effective performance of both the board and the president is mutual cooperation: the trustees should support and have confidence in the president, and the president should provide a staff support system for individual trustees as well as the chairman.

To ensure continuing effectiveness, regular evaluation of the board and board policies should be planned. Time on the board agenda should be reserved annually for appraisal, and at that time the directors should submit their critiques of the past year's performance. A committee on board performance may be established to recommend improvements, with the chairman playing a key role in the evaluation process. The board should also call for, and approve, evaluation systems throughout the organization—systems that identify individual performance and allow appropriate reward.

The board must also establish regeneration capabilities. A plan should be developed for filling a vacancy in the presidency. A procedure should also be established for the identification of individual board talent, and a balanced process should be established to select new trustees. An orientation program for new trustees should be designed.

A COEL (New York State Regents Advisory Committee on Educational Leadership, April 1965) survey shows that new trustees are usually leaders in their own occupational fields but that their leadership ability may not be immediately transferable to the educational enterprise. About half of those trustees surveyed had no prior educational experience, yet only 6 percent reported having been offered special sessions or programs for orientation. The orientation program should be devoted to guiding and developing the leadership talents that trustees bring to the educational board. A contemporary set of bylaws will also help the board accomplish its objectives. The trustees should develop and approve bylaws covering such topics as legal basis and authority; elections; board membership (number and terms, qualifications, geographical distribution, nominations, authority, and filling vacancies); the board as an organization (annual meeting, officers of the board, terms of office, duties of officers, consultants to the board, and committee structure); and meetings (regular and special meetings, preparation for meeting, order of business, parliamentary procedures, authority to conduct business, citizen participation, and quorum). Trustees must assume the basic responsibility for the soundness of the financial condition of the institution and allocate decision-making authority in accordance with competence. The board should also provide for effective governance and approve the organizational structure.

Trustees must develop a common understanding of organizational objectives and then establish a planning framework in which trustees, administrators, and staff can each play a significant role. In this way, the energies of the professionals produce maximum results, and the other resources of the institution are optimally allocated. The trustees must question the contribution of every new program and every old program to the fulfillment of the goals of the institution.

Trustees and top executives of educational institutions usually do not reach general consensus on the outstanding features or definitions of a policy. A policy is a written statement of an organization's intent or direction based on a philosophy or belief that guides the actions of people in the organization. Policies should be written, approved at the highest level of the organization, enforced, and extend over long periods of time. Their formulation requires previous study and thought so that they deal with important matters rather than detail. Experience has shown that, in matters of policy formulation and execution, an informed group is better than an individual for providing the balanced thought and judgment needed to set particular goals of organizational performance. The board should supply this group thinking and judgment. However, execution is best performed by the strong individual leadership supplied by the college president. He or his staff can initiate and recommend organization policy also. In some cases, the role of the board may be limited to identifying the need for policy or asking the president or a committee of the board to study a problem; draft recommendations; and review, modify, and approve recommended policies.

There is often confusion between the policy-making role

of the board and the degree to which a board should be involved in the management of an organization. The line of demarcation is gray. Perhaps, each trustee should ask himself how the board can best fulfill its responsibilities for management. The board may possibly be no more than an observer of the scene or an auditor with no special operational responsibilities. However, the policy makers cannot consider themselves responsible for managing to any large extent in an enterprise and do so little. A board must do more than merely sit on the top rung of the ladder of an organization, hire a chief executive, and watch him manage. The complexity of the educational establishment demands far more. Boards must demand complete planning proposals, a review of performance and plans, a proper approach to decision-making, answers to discerning questions, and individual independence in thought. An effective board holds the responsibility for the enterprise as a whole. Therefore, it must work closely with management and make decisions in a number of specific areas. One of the prime responsibilities is assuring that planning and decision-making are effective. A board must remember that decision-making requires rational action—action that should lead effectively and efficiently to a preselected goal. There can be no rational action without a clear goal, a clear understanding of alternatives for reaching the goal, an adequate analysis of alternatives in terms of the goal, and a desire to optimize the use of resources in reaching the goal.

Another reason trustees fail to perform as they should is that they do not know what is expected of them. Personal guidelines for trustee behavior should be created by the board members with counsel from the president and should be presented to prospective trustees for their consideration before they accept the appointment or run for office. It should also be the central part of the orientation program for new trustees.

The trustee should attend all meetings, read the agenda

and all accompanying materials well in advance of the meeting, and seek further information before the meeting if advance materials are not sufficiently comprehensive. During meetings, the trustee should not allow issues to be rushed through and brought to a quick vote because of lack of time. All major policy questions should be first explored in committee and then considered by the board with at least one meeting between presentation of the committee recommendation and the vote. If financial or technical subjects need further clarification, the trustee should speak up and ask for an explanation.

The trustee should be expected to draw upon his personal experience to help the board and the college. He should use personal contacts to help raise funds or meet special college needs. In social situations he should ask for advice and opinions about the college for continuous community feedback. To become familiar with the campus, its growth, and its master plan, the trustee should become personally acquainted with as many administrators and faculty as possible and should occasionally attend campus activities. He should keep abreast of current legislation regarding funding, student rights, liability, and other matters and should keep abreast of all aspects of trusteeship by reading appropriate professional journals regularly. He should represent the campus to the community by being available for public speaking engagements and participation in planning groups and other community activities. If the trustee is unable to perform 90 percent of these functions he should resign from the board.

Board effectiveness is allied to the competence of the chairman (see implementation section, p. 154). The chairman must maintain good relationships with governmental units, the college staff, the press, and the public in general. He must often serve as a catalyst for the board—suggesting and developing in-service training for board members, stimulating their individual talents, appointing board committees and calling for their performance and reports, and initiating performance evaluation of top executives as well as of the board. He must cooperate and participate with the trustees in the conduct of organizational affairs and should be expected to handle special requests and carry out special assignments on behalf of the board. The chairman should also recognize his function as a coach: to expedite decision-making and voting after due deliberation, to help dissenting members accept the majority rule, and to consult with trustees who are not carrying out their responsibilities or who are violating board bylaws and practices.

The subject of trustee effectiveness need not be a source of embarrassment for administrators or boards when approached in a straightforward manner. Performance standards as described in the foregoing passages should be helpful. When the board establishes its standards and initiates programs for involving all trustees actively, the board function becomes dynamic rather than static. The results are felt throughout the entire organization if the administration and teaching staffs are able to work with plans they helped create and know that the trustees, too, are expected to meet certain standards. In today's swiftly changing educational climate there is no room for board members who are content merely to attend meetings and hold title to the position. Essential requirements for an effective board are the desire to be effective; clear identification of fundamental responsibilities, duties, and expected accomplishments; comprehension of the board's overall role in the operation of the organization; understanding of what management is and does; selection of an effective chairman; use of intelligence, experience in problem-solving, and independent thinking; expectations for efficiency in operating the governing body; recognition of the grave responsibilities inherent in being the extreme top level of the organization and of the fact that the manner in which this level operates directly affects the performance and morale of all personnel; and knowledge of where the organization is going, how it will get there, whether it is doing the best possible job and utilizing its human and material resources in the best interests of students and society. There is very little doubt that the most effective organizations today have, in addition to effective management teams, capable trustees at the helm.

Chapter 4

Management Development

That educational management lacks management skills and systems does not necessarily imply a lack of formal education. A manager and his effectiveness on the job cannot be predicted by the number of degrees he holds, the grades he received, the institutions he attended, or the number of books he has written. Indeed, it seems almost hypocritical that educators can talk about management and management skills in their schools of industrial relations and schools of business but seem unable to apply the processes they teach to increase the health and productivity of their own organizations. Educators must learn to probe all possible means of maximizing the resources at their disposal, and the business world and its managerial expertise may be helpful. Although business does not have all the answers, it has made greater strides toward finding the answers to avoid failure. Of significance are the reasons businesses, like educational organizations, do fail. A comprehensive study by Dun & Bradstreet, Inc., surveyed corporations that did not succeed for answers to the question,

"What caused 10,326 businesses to fail in 1971?" Underlying causes which received highest percentages were incompetence, unbalanced experience, and lack of managerial experience. The question may well be "What caused educational institutions to fail in 1971?"

Those individuals with the ability to understand human behavior and apply proper managerial concepts to produce desired results are certainly sought after today by educational and business organizations. Though the critical shortage of competent managerial talent is a problem as acute in the field of higher education as it is in industry, educators are running significantly behind in attempts to deal with the problem.

Top industrial organizations have found one solution to their problem by providing extensive in-service development of their own potential management talent, requiring commitment in terms of organizational priorities and resources. Higher education has largely ignored this concept; the primary source for filling key managerial positions is untrained, upwardly mobile academicians who take their turn in the classroom and then become a part of the higher education establishment. This source of leadership leaves much to be desired and results in administrators who come to their posts as amateurs, lacking management skills and the knowledge of application to management systems. For example, the selection of a division chairman or department chairman for a typical academic institution proceeds with the supervisor searching the faculty roster for one or two outstanding teachers who have already been "mentally tapped" as candidates. Too often, the candidate accepts the managerial post because he thinks it will bring him more money and prestige, more fringe benefits, and an image of success. In reality, the instructor who has been a leader and motivator of students in a classroom setting has

34

accepted a managerial challenge about which he knows and understands very little.

That the instructor has accepted the job for the wrong reasons may, in large part, be the fault of the organization. How often is a likely candidate told that to become a manager he must become a generalist and no longer be a specialist in his field? That higher salary, status, and power will not ensure long-term satisfaction, much less effectiveness, in the managerial role? That the real reward will be getting things done through and with people?

The instructor undoubtedly has great skills for teaching students, but these same skills do not arm him adequately to be a manager. He experiences frustration and confusion in working with his staff; he stumbles through the new processes of evaluation, budget cutting, delegating, personnel selection, coaching, appraising, making decisions, and resolving conflicts; he questions the scope of his managerial job, and a contemporary job description is lacking.

There is at present a critical shortage of competent managers in the field of education, and the need for well-trained managers is going to increase drastically. The primary source of administrators will be upwardly mobile academicians, and these recruits lack experience and training in the managerial skills. It becomes apparent that the responsibility is to assist their travel upward with a vehicle of management development programs. Measures are needed to shuck the old methods in which selection is made from people who were never equipped to be managers, and in those cases where there is dormant and undeveloped potential, some tool must be designed to develop the talent.

The only truly effective development program is a systematic one that produces obvious and needed change. A development program cannot be superimposed upon an institution; it must be custom designed to the specific needs of that organization. Although models are available whose initial planning reflects an understanding of the common areas of managerial weakness prevalent in administration, it will be imperative that the elemental differences of each institution be taken into consideration.

Managerial training, as a crucial part of development, must be based on a continuous search for better ways to fulfill the objectives of the organization. The growth and successful maturation of an organization are affected by the management behavior (tools, techniques, and know-how) within the organization. Figure 1 shows how growth will be either a process of maturation or a process of decline, depending upon managerial behavior. After the critical period the organization either continues in an upward or maturing period or, if the appropriate managerial processes have not been applied, declines toward possible failure.

A synopsis of an administrative development program that could be implemented by a two-year institution is as follows. The effort begins with the appointment of a committee from the administration aided by the president and perhaps a professional consultant to study and define development objectives and to plan the program. These initial steps require the better part of an academic year, after which the following objectives are presented: to increase understanding of the dynamics of organizations and of relationships between the individual administrator and the overall organization; to increase understanding of the functions and purposes of management within an educational organization; to increase among administrators acceptance of the assumption that good management practices complement the goals of an educational organization; to increase the motivation of the individual administrator to improve his own performance; to increase the readiness of the individual to accept change and to encourage innovation; to upgrade administrative skills, management tech-

Management Development

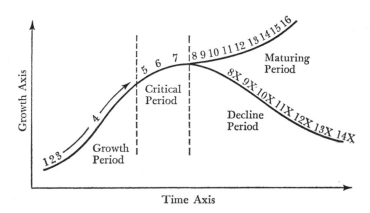

FIGURE 1. Organizational growth versus managerial behavior. Growth period: (1) initiative, (2) vision, (3) determined leadership, (4) begins to vary leadership and managerial style with growth. Critical period: (5) plays hunches, (6) rewards loyalty, (7) not developing crucial subordinates. Maturing period: (8) delegation, (9) team work, (10) planning, (11) controls, (12) enlightened leadership, (13) evaluation, (14) OD, (15) goals—MBO, (16) problem analysis—conflict resolution. Decline period: (8X) no controls, (9X) no management development, (10X) management by crisis, (11X) weak subordinates, (12X) no teamwork, (13X) high turnover, (14X) no delegation.

niques, and leadership abilities; and to increase confidence in the institution's interest in and commitment to the development and promotability of its administrators.

A two-phase program is planned. During the first phase, monthly seminars are held to sensitize administrators to principles of management and fundamental management processes. The second phase of the program also might span a year, stressing individual analysis, personal goal setting and accomplishment, and the application of principles of manage-

37

ment—the self-development of each administrator. It is a continuous program.

In planning seminars for the first phase, program planners are cautioned to solicit the best qualified experts as seminar leaders, drawing from such resources as management institutes at major universities, and to be specific in communicating the objectives of the proposed seminar to those experts. A committee is formed to work with each seminar leader to develop materials realistic to proposed application of the development program including special case studies, group involvement techniques, visual aids, role playing, and other stimulating learning activities. Seminar leaders are asked to suggest current literature that could be provided to participants in advance of the meeting. Participants are also requested to perform certain activities prior to the session, for example, to provide examples of current motivation problems with which they are confronted.

An evaluation form is used by participants for all sessions, and if these evaluations indicate the need, the content of sessions can be changed. Seminar leaders are also asked for their evaluations and suggestions, and a periodic evaluation is planned for the overall program. As many individuals as possible are involved in the planning and arrangements for the sessions.

The seminar is not to be the final activity on a topic. Follow-up studies or small group sessions are planned to implement ideas presented at seminars. A file of management materials is available to personnel, and a suggested reading list is continuously updated.

This type of administrative development is not impossible to achieve. Of importance is understanding the role and definition of a manager. A manager is one who is entrusted with the responsibilities for utilizing efficiently and effectively the many resources available to him such as money, facilities, manpower, time, equipment, people, and their relationships; who is able to confidently employ appropriate processes to reap productive results; who gets genuine satisfaction from being able to successfully influence others to perform willingly; and who can stimulate others to achieve even better results.

The qualifications necessary for the person in a top administrative post are: power with people, intelligence, flexibility, guts, integrity, confidence, and inner drive. He must be able to learn, think, and understand quickly; make sound judgments and decisions; communicate effectively; act vigorously and react quickly; and get along with, understand, and get things done through others. He must be able to lead, plan, organize, delegate, and control and must possess a knowledge of finance, empathy, and a certain amount of charisma or personal charm. He must be a generalist rather than a specialist; he must be innovative, creative, able to benefit from experience, and able to shoot for the long-range target. The administrator must not only manage better and differently and skillfully delegate the day-to-day functions to subordinates, but he must also remain informed, shifting gears as demanded by the changing of the organization.

The growing and maturing organization manifests changing needs—more people, more complex jobs, greater need for communication and coordination—that must be met if the organization is to continue in an upward maturation progression. The same criteria necessary to launch the organization—the enthusiam, the energy, the sense of initiating a mission—may not be those necessary to continue its successful survival. The organization reaches a critical point where the courageous initiative, vision to conceive, and determination to persist must be replaced with stable and strategic direction rather than original new thrusts. It must be guided by planned growth rather than free-lance inspiration.

Another aspect for consideration in a development

program is the delegation process. One of the greatest shortcomings of newly appointed managers is the inability to distinguish between managing and operating. Daily operating decisions and tasks should not consume the time of executive managers skilled in the art of delegation. Authority, responsibility, and accountability relate to managerial position in the hierarchy, and appropriate feedback should verify that tasks have been done at the appropriate personnel level and at a given quality level without the personal involvement of the administrator.

The administrator skilled in the art of delegation asks himself the following questions prior to assigning work tasks to a subordinate: Is he alert enough to handle the job, sufficiently motivated, able to get the cooperation he needs? Does he have enough self-confidence? Will the job assignment, if given to him, create frictions? Does he need more development? Knowing what to delegate, and to whom, is important in order that delegated tasks tap the most able human talent as well as combine achievement of organization goals and fulfillment of human needs. Understanding and practicing the skillful art of delegation results in more effective use of time and serves to alleviate an unwillingness to delegate at all or the extreme of overdelegation or too high an expectation of the subordinate by the supervisor.

Another factor to be assessed in developing management is the effective management of time. The use of time is significantly related to setting objectives and designing the means to reach them. The ineffective utilization of time frequently results from a weakness in delegating authority, particularly in feedback systems that verify that a job was well done without the administrator having to personally check it. Managers must learn to identify and understand how time is currently used and where the waste is. Systematizing work, organizing working materials, and striving for orderliness set the stage for efficiency. Managers could reap more productivity in some cases, however, if they dared to stop fighting the clock and to judge administrative work by results achieved.

Additional methods for assessing use of time are work sampling studies, worksheets, random observations, charting time usage, hour by hour analysis, and daytime scheduling.

The percentage of time an administrator spends in actual management is a direct gauge of effective use of his time. The chief administrator of an institution, for example, should devote most of his time and energy to institutional planning and development. Conversely, a department chairman would probably spend the greater share of his time teaching (operating) and a much lower share of his time planning and administering for his department.

The appraisal process is another managerial technique utilized to aid individual skill growth and to assist the individual in the modification of his behavior, if necessary, in order to be more effective in his job. The appraisal process, if not used correctly, can harm more than help the relationship between subordinate and supervisor. Inadequate appraisal methods are critical and advisory, emphasize the subordinate's weaknesses and failures, and attempt to counsel him. The appraisal process, like many other processes, is at the mercy of its user. It should be considered a personal development tool to aid the subordinate in his professional growth and to help him become increasingly skillful and effective in the job assigned. Its primary function should be to assist the employee in maintaining a satisfactory performance on his present job through better understanding of the supervisor–employee relationship through the opportunities of talking and consulting with his supervisor. In another sense the appraisal process may be considered a personal management tool providing assistance in making decisions leading to promotion, salary increases, transfer, or suggested release. Qualified appraisers can achieve results beneficial to all concerned; incompetent appraising is cause for failure of the process and alienation of employees.

Too often a gap exists between what the supervisor feels a job is and what the subordinate perceives a job to be. Therefore, it is important to set the stage for coaching and development. Carefully defining the job, determining accountability and standards of performance, and then securing mutual agreement on results desired is a helpful approach to closing the gap. The supervisor as a coach and consultant helps the subordinate do his job better and encourages him to excel; gives the subordinate a clear picture of how well he is doing and expresses appreciation for work well done; builds strong supervisor–subordinate rapport by open communication, feedback, listening to problems, and alleviating anxieties; and initiates the development of plans jointly with the subordinate to improve his total abilities.

The failure of the manager to coach often becomes a primary reason for failure in performance among subordinates. The success of coaching depends in large part on the preparation of both supervisor and subordinate and on the climate established for the coaching procedure. Information about the subordinate's job performance, resource materials that constructively aid in improving performance, and a general attitude of concern and cooperation are all assets for the coach. The subordinate must be encouraged to reflect on his job performance and criteria affecting it and be made to feel that the coaching procedure is for his personal benefit.

The selection of personnel represents a critical process for any organization, particularly for the community college. Too often the most common criteria for top leadership posts are academic degrees, experience, evidence of status, research, publications, and recognition in the field; there is often little emphasis on the applicant's management ability or knowledge and execution of good management practices. A patterned inter-

42

view is most critical in the selection process, and elements to be assessed are work record, military service record, schooling, early home environment, domestic status, financial status, health condition, character traits, motivation, level of energy, and emotional maturity.

As a preparatory step to the interview, background information on the candidate and a plan for the interview assist in providing an accurate picture of the whole person. The interviewer must also sharpen his communication skills, the most difficult to learn but most important being the art of listening. The interviewer must overcome the tendency to begin thinking about his next question without listening to the applicant's responses. When this happens the interviewer misses cues and valuable information.

Effective decision-making is an ability that most educational managers need to develop or strengthen. Common weaknesses in the decision-making process are uncertainty as to who is responsible for making what decisions and lack of adequate information for making decisions. Within the framework of the objective decision-making process, first consideration must be given to needs and objectives relating to the situation. The "absolutes" and the "desirables" may then be categorized. Objectivity and control of bias are necessary for sound decision-making. Also very important is the impact of decisions made in the present but to be implemented in the future. A quantitative scheme for calculating the probability of trouble would be helpful in the selection of alternatives and considerations for implementation. Decision-making can be strengthened and developed when it is fully understood in its relation to the management process and the organizational purposes.

Conflict resolution and problem solving are also assets with which a manager must arm himself. Where there are people there will be problems, no matter how discreet or discerning management has been; constructing ways of controlling and minimizing problems may well produce a climate of lower incidence. Problem solving may take various forms—counseling, grievance procedure, or disciplinary action. The patience and kindness approach can be costly to the organization; third party resolution is time-consuming; and disciplinary measures can be dictatorial and destructive of morale. Each method warrants close inspection for the particular case at hand.

Regardless of the nature of the problem there must be an established pattern for coping, and there must be action taken to listen, release the emotion, and reduce the tension. Rational examination can then determine how severe and realistic the problem is and find alternative ways of resolving it. Most important, the course of resolution to be followed must be justifiable for that particular problem.

Motivation, the driving force that influences people to greater achievement or persuades them to make changes or respond, is another consideration. Motivation as an internal drive comes more easily within a newly established, rapidly growing organization where there is an atmosphere of excitement and challenge. When organizational growth reaches a stage of relative stability or maturity, however, motivation ceases to be self-generating and becomes increasingly dependent on external forces such as skill of supervision.

That divergent motivational forces may exist (organization versus individual) highlights the need for better understanding of the relationships between personal motivation and organizational goal attainment and the need to improve management methods that foster compatibility. What an organization needs to fulfill its commitments cannot be continuously in conflict with what is considered personally satisfying to the worker in his job setting. There is evidence that the application of behavioral science theories to industry is a positive step toward motivating the worker within the context of overall organizational well-being, a step that educational management could well afford to explore. Developmental efforts in this area could have great impact on employee relations.

A dynamic manager strives for the reinforcement of creative behavior for building creative organizations. Two of the many facets of the creative approach by management are highlighted. First, individuals are inclined to reject ideas or potential solutions and thereby destroy the creative environment.

Second, creativity can be encouraged as a result of systematic processes. For example, brainstorming, a practice long used in business and industry, is a healthy exploration technique which generates new and unusual ideas. "Synectics theory applies to the integration of diverse individuals into a problem-stating, problem-solving group. It is an operational theory for the conscious use of the preconscious psychological mechanisms present in man's creative activity. The purpose of developing such a theory is to increase the probability of success in problem-stating, problem-solving situations" (Gordon, 1961, p. 3).

Operations research is not as well understood in academic circles as it should be. Community colleges are weak in experimental design, methods of research, and objective evaluation. This is not a criticism but a statement of fact resulting from the kinds of people who are employed. Being primarily teaching-oriented, faculties have not had appropriate experience in research and need help in understanding its importance and methodology in order that it is not neglected.

Community college spokesmen are often guilty of making many more claims than they can validate by objective research. They are vulnerable when accountability is called for by local citizens, legislators, state offices, or federal bureaucracies. The community college has for a decade or more been studied, surveyed, and observed by many, sometimes competently and effectively. Many of these studies have been helpful to the development of the community college during its early years, but as it reaches maturity and continues in the competition for state and national resources, there will be scouts looking for its most vulnerable weaknesses. Limited or poor data to justify its positions will be a poor line of defense.

The tendency to reduce support for research may be caused by four factors: the mission of institutional research is misunderstood; institutional research is structured inconsistently with top management goals; institutional research is staffed incompetently; and institutional research is researching the wrong priorities. Considering the state of the art of institutional research in higher education today, it should not be surprising that critics are asking significant questions about the results and efficiency of operation in the higher educational institutions. Until higher education begins to fill in some of the neglected areas of institutional research, the credibility gap between academe and the public will continue to exist.

Research, of course, is not everything. But research leads to direction, and direction leads to commitment. In order for significant research to take place, those involved must understand its function and value the use of data in decision-making. Those doing the research must be trusted and respected, be able to establish and maintain cooperative working relationships, and be able to anticipate problems before they occur. There must be access to knowledge of current problems and issues so that timely data may be forthcoming. Objectivity and detachment warrant reemphasis, and skills in quantitative methods and research methodology are additional requirements. Effective oral and written communication are paramount.

The cry for accountability, for outcome measurement and evaluation, from local citizens and state and federal governments mandates the need for making plans and decisions in terms of the outcomes desired. There must be a linkage between the resources used and the results achieved; the output must justify the input in higher education. Planners and decision makers, not researchers, must take the lead in establishing this balance. Education has been very cost conscious: decisions have been made primarily on the basis of how much something costs, regardless of the outcome.

Private organizational evaluation has traditionally been based on such end results as production, sales, profits, and percentage of net earnings to sales. But such standards of evaluation are not applicable in the field of higher education. How does a college measure its production or its profits? The community college needs more exact measurements and standards of performance not only to evaluate the outcomes but to provide a more accurate means for planning future activities and calculating modifications. Criteria for continued, if not initial, consideration are: the impact of the institution on the student (whether the institution does for the student what it is supposed to); institutional dynamics (how well the working parts relate to each other)—the effectiveness of goal-setting, decision-making, policy-making, planning, and budgeting and how they relate to the final outcome; the form and structure of the institution (the effectiveness of the board, administration, and faculty and their ability to communicate to allow desired outcomes to take place); and quality control and the efficiency of budgeting practices in relationship to the outcome (whether the student got his money's worth).

Effective wage and salary administration is another facet in management development worthy of priority. Reward for service whether by direct or indirect means encompasses a wide battery of considerations. Compensation decisions may become so complex and varied that a systematic approach to each is necessary and would include an integrated analysis of the theory, policy, and practice of that particular facet of wage and salary administration.

The search for solutions to compensation problems has not outdistanced the changes taking place in the problems. Compensation has become a much broader term, covering direct remuneration as well as fringe benefits and nonfinancial rewards. The nature of the work forces, the integration of theory and practice in compensation, and the agencies that influence and are influenced by the general acceptance of a wide number of compensation practices are all changing. That a proven precut pattern exists to fit each compensation problem is wishful thinking. However, rational analysis of each problem must be viewed in sociological, psychological, political, ethical, and economic terms, and decisions will be subject to various tests from various sources. The question of pay and its effective administration is complex and difficult to standardize.

Objectives of a good wage and salary program will provide an orderly procedure for expenditure of a major portion of an operational budget (retain, secure, and advance employees); maintain a competitive position in the labor market from which employees are obtained; maintain a desirable relation between staff costs and other budgeted items within each department of the organization; realize maximum return from personnel expenditures; provide equal pay for equal work throughout the organization; provide a positive and consistent relationship between salary increases and identifiable performance on the job; and aid the departments in doing a better job in personnel management.

Wage and salary administration is detailed later in this book, and despite the various controversies and searches for better solutions, organizations will doubtless continue to provide compensation in whatever form appears to provide motivation.

Management Development

Collective bargaining is a trend of our times to be faced squarely and analytically. Elements of the bargaining process that must be understood and discussed by management prior to possible confrontations are the recognition process, setting up a negotiating committee, preparing for the sessions, techniques of negotiating, conduct at the bargaining table, content and scope of the agreement, impasse procedures, preserving management's rights, and implementing and living with the agreement. Higher education management must not be fearful of but prepared for collective bargaining. While employees engage in collective bargaining, management must engage in productivity bargaining, which means increased productivity in relation to dollars spent.

Higher education management has been carefree in its approach to long-range planning. Two-year colleges cannot afford to approach planning carelessly, although this approach may stem from a lack of good planning principles and models for carrying out the process. Ewing (1972) defines long-range planning as the "continuous process of making . . . (risk-taking) decisions systematically and with the best possible knowledge of their futurity, organizing systematically the efforts needed to carry out these decisions, and measuring the results of these decisions against the expectations through organized, systematic feedback." Management has the responsibility for this risk-taking, decision-making venture. Some basic requirements for the process are specific knowledge of the nature, function, and purpose of the organization; knowledge of basic theory and concepts; and a step-by-step, rational approach.

Long-range planning is not foretelling the future; it is not a future decision-maker nor an eliminator of risks. Long-range planning does not decide what will be done tomorrow but makes decisions now that bring results in the future. It initiates action now in order to cope adequately with the uncertainities of the future.

Budgeting has been handled predominantly as a process of addition or multiplication; some critics have described it as creeping incrementalism. This conventional approach has used student growth as the justification for budget increases. Planning, goal-setting, priorities, evaluation—elements mentioned often before—again need to play a much greater role in the budgeting process. All institutions are faced with the necessity of more effective budgeting procedures to take into account new limitations of financial resources in the preparation of annual operating budgets.

Inherent in traditional budgeting practice are deficiencies that limit its effectiveness. The programs of the higher educational institution must be dynamic and responsive to change (in interests, concerns, and job market), to growth, and to the advances in knowledge. Budgeting procedures that produce flexibility and more effective controls and cause old ideas to compete with new are demanded at a time of financial crisis and minimal public confidence.

If an institution is to remain dynamic, financial resources must be made available to develop new programs or augment present ones in response to the changing needs, even if this provision necessitates cutbacks or elimination of some programs. Strategies that allow more flexibility are consolidating several programs, readjusting present programs to fit present needs, percentage cutbacks across the board, cooperative arrangements with other appropriate institutions to offer given programs, requiring each plan of expansion to solicit its own financial resources, and allocating vacated positions back to the central administration for reassignment on the basis of greatest need.

To improve the budgeting process, administrators must

constantly evaluate the alternative uses of available resources in a systematic manner, and courses of action must continue to promote the overall goals of the institution at minimum cost.

Educational institutions, like other organizations, attempt to maximize output and minimize cost by applying management systems. In recent years there have been a growing number of systems aimed at helping the management process. Some are more complex than others and require more study and discussion before implementation. Some of the more noteworthy systems are described here.

PPBS (Planning, Programming, and Budgeting System) is a process that strengthens an organization's capability to do long-range planning and helps management use available resources in the most effective way to meet planned goals. PPBS establishes and makes explicit the relationships among the organization's objectives, its programs and activities, the resource implications of those activities, and their financial expression in a budget. Much information needed for rational planning is thereby provided in easily useable form. PPBS contributes directly to management decision-making by providing analyses of the consequences, in terms of estimated costs and expected benefits, of possible program decisions. It is primarily an instrument for overall planning that uses existing systems for directing and controlling operations; it is specifically designed for long-range planning and budgeting; and it stresses the use of quantitative analytical methods.

PERT (Program Evaluation and Review Technique) acts as a managerial tool for defining and coordinating what must be done to successfully accomplish objectives on time.

OD (Organization Development) is a strategy to change the structure of an organization, its beliefs, its attitutudes, and its values so that it can more successfully cope with the challenge of new technologies and change itself.

MBO (Management by Objectives) as defined by Odiorne (1965) is a "process whereby the superior and the subordinate managers of an enterprise jointly identify its common goals, define each individual's major areas of responsibility in terms of the results expected of him, and use these measures as guides for operating the unit and assessing the contribution of each of its members." It is to this system that this book primarily addresses itself.

Chapter 5

Management by Objectives in the Two-Year College

Management development alone cannot ensure that an organization maintains good health and copes with change. In addition managers must understand and utilize the concept of organizational development (OD) as a means of accomplishing organizational change. Organizational development as defined by one authority (Bennis, 1969) is "a response to change, a complex educational strategy intended to change beliefs, attitudes, values, and structure of organizations so that they can better adapt to new technologies, markets, and challenges, and the dizzying rate of change itself." Another source (Beckhard, 1969) defines organizational development as "an effort (1) planned, (2) organization-wide, (3) managed from the top, to (4) increase organization effectiveness and health through (5) planned interventions in the organization's 'processes,' using behavioral science knowledge."

Behavioral science hypotheses underlying the theory of organization development are that people have a drive toward growth and self-realization. Work organized to meet people's needs as well as to achieve organizational requirements tends to produce the highest productivity and quality of production. Persons in groups that go through a managed process of increasing openness about positive and negative feelings develop a strong identification with the goals of the group and its other members. The group becomes increasingly capable of dealing constructively with potentially disruptive issues. The ability to be flexible and responsible flows naturally from groups that feel a common identification and an ability to influence their environment.

Organizational development begins with a process of diagnosing the roadblocks that prevent the release of human potential within the organization; objectives are then formulated to eliminate and minimize these roadblocks. To create an open, problem-solving climate; to supplement authority with knowledge and competence; to locate decision-making and problem-solving responsibilities as close to the information sources as possible; and to build trust among individuals and groups are all objectives of organizational development. Additional objectives are to make competition more relevant to work goals and to maximize collaborative efforts; to develop a reward system that recognizes both the achievement of the organization and personal development; to increase the sense of sharing of organization objectives throughout the organization; to help managers to manage according to objectives peripheral to their areas of responsibility; and to increase the self-control and self-direction of people within the organization. Through a planned strategy, OD should enable the two-year college to examine critically its managerial practices; investigate present structure for effectiveness; and initiate appropriate action to improve intergroup collaboration, planning, communication, and motivation.

A management system that has been successfully used by business and industrial organizations is management by objectives (MBO), which has great potential as a system to be implemented in the two-year college. Its focus is to enable the institution, significant subunits, and employees to manage work more efficiently against defined goals and plans.

Management by objectives is described by one expert (Odiorne, 1965) as a system for making organizational structure work, to bring about vitality and personal involvement in the hierarchy by means of statements of what is expected for everyone involved and measurement of what is actually achieved, and stressing ability and achievements rather than personality. Another source (Deegan, n.d.) defines management by objectives as "a continual process whereby superior and subordinate managers of the firm periodically identify its common goals, define each individual's major area of responsibility in terms of results expected of him, and use these agreed-upon measures as guides for operating each department and for assessing the contribution of each manager to the work of the entire company." Two concepts common to all MBO programs are that the clearer the idea one has of what one is trying to accomplish, the greater the chances of accomplishing it and that progress can only be measured in terms of a goal. These concepts are merely logical extensions of the normal management functions, planning and control. However, the difference brought about by MBO is the rigor with which planning and control are carried out. Constant effort is directed toward the improvement of the planning process.

Management by objectives as discussed by Drucker (1954) and systematized by Odiorne (1965) came about as an answer to management needs. Private industry and business as well as education are wrestling with the problem of holding costs down by stabilizing or increasing the productivity of workers. MBO improves motivation by involving each individual in the establishment of his own goals to be approved or modified by his superior.

Research has shown that the lack of communication between superior and subordinate often accounts for the gap between a worker's performance and his boss' expectations. Properly applied, MBO forces more communication between managers. The system acknowledges individual expertise and departmental orientation, yet forces coordination of efforts. The management team sets objectives for the whole before delineating specific goals for subunits, thus fitting all of the parts together.

MBO is based on participation and interaction and should support a creative environment. It seeks personal involvement in the functions of the organization and is oriented toward the fullest realization of individual potential in the success of the organization. The individual is motivated through his understanding of what the organization is trying to accomplish and his relationship to those goals. It helps relieve his feeling of being merely a number on a payroll and makes him feel a vital part of the whole organizational structure with a voice in its operation and a commitment to its success. For example, an individual worker and his supervisor set mutually agreed-upon goals. This in itself is a motivating device. As an author of the goals, the worker feels vitally involved, understands their importance to the organization, believes in them, feels an ownership of them, and is challenged to make them a reality.

The system reinforces the principle of obtaining the best efforts from both the individual workers and from the managers of the working groups. MBO permits greater control of managers over their operations and encourages improved subordinate-superior relationships as a result of joint participation in goal-setting and planning.

MBO has potential for minimizing many of the criticisms of higher education, particularly that there is little agreement about priorities and goals. Private organizations attempt to ensure that the goals of individual managers blend into a matrix of mutual compatibility and supportiveness, a phenomenon equally necessary in the two-year college. The primary advantage of the system is better performance; organizations are more likely to achieve whatever they set out to achieve if the system helps them to understand specifically what it is they want and need. Additionally, control is easier; MBO provides a better basis for keeping track of progress because goals and means are clearly understood. When something goes wrong, management knows about it quickly. Control is over operations rather than people, and people are motivated to operate in the direction of established goals.

MBO is most effective when implemented from top management through the first line of supervision, provided that top management is committed to and supportive of the system. A well planned strategy involving key subordinates is fundamental to assess the readiness of an organization for MBO and to establish a judicious implementation schedule. A climate of trust, readiness, and enthusiasm on the part of the institutional managers will best nourish successful implementation. A significant number of managers must feel the need to make the organizational climate more consistent with both individual and environmental needs, to change cultural norms, to change structure and roles, to improve intergroup collaboration, to open up communications, to plan better, and to improve motivation of the work force.

Following preliminary review, the MBO system may dictate such basic change to the organization as greater delegation of authority, greater information flow, larger budget for the management process, change in salary and bonus procedures, and the creation or updating of job descriptions. The system can be and is utilized by some organizations in limited application as an approach only for performance appraisal, a compensation program, or another single phase. Most organizations that have attempted partial utilization have learned through experience that limited application within the total framework of a more traditional system of management reduces the potential effectiveness of the MBO system. For some organizations, however, such limited application presents a starting point for initiating the system on an organization-wide basis. Such initiation, as a forerunner to total implementation, can provide a way of introducing concepts and developing skills essential to the system.

After readiness has been established, the implementation of a management by objectives system in the two-year college should take certain specific steps.

First, the central purpose and function of the organization must be generally understood and agreed upon. The general public does not necessarily understand the central purpose and function of the education organization, and activities of constituencies within that organization leave some doubt as to its basic mission. For example, the universities, which often engage in the threefold function of teaching, research, and transmission of knowledge, have lost some degree of credibility because of criticism for overindulging in government contracts or national defense research to the extent that dissenting students complained for a lack of instruction. Students, and often the general public whose offspring are the students, believe that the primary function of the university is to teach students and not compromise them to research, consulting, or government contracts. Likewise, the community college must carefully delineate its purpose and function to be unique from the four-year college and must do so in such a manner that the public will understand explicitly what its purposes and functions are. The MBO system forces the organization and its components to place the intended mission of the organization at the most visible point of observation. A mission statement, for example, may say: "The mission of College Y is to provide the highest quality community college program of education designed to offer each student maximum opportunity to learn and develop; to seek out the most modern, creative, and effective organizational and educational ideas; and to test, improve, and implement those ideas that meet the needs of the community at a reasonable cost."

The establishment of the central purpose and function of the organization is the responsibility of management and the board. A representative group of the organization must be involved in refining this statement in order to gain general constituency support. The chief executive officer and the board finally approve the mission statement and take action to commit the organization to it. The importance of full subscription to the mission statement by board, chief executive, and constituencies cannot be overemphasized; the mission statement becomes the measure by which all subunit purposes and objectives are appropriated for commitment.

Secondly, the institutional goals for the specific year must be drawn up and agreed upon by a significant number of the organization's constituencies. After the central purposes and function of the organization have been established, there must follow a statement of goals for the coming year, identified as preliminary institutional goals and initiated at the executive management level. All ideas and initial input are combined into a position statement that includes suggested priorities for the goals. This document is made available to all levels of the organization along with communication soliciting discussion, additions, and revisions with supporting information. This solicitous process helps to establish a feeling of ownership in the organization and commitment to its goals. Management must make a sincere effort to review in detail suggestions and modifications and incorporate those practical and significant to the goal-setting process for that year.

A second draft of institutional goals integrating the new information is distributed to the constituencies for further communicative review. Where possible, detailed feedback should explain why the first suggestions or revisions were not integrated into the second draft of the goal statements. After reasonable time has elapsed and discussion has again taken place, a second solicitation is made by top management for the purpose of reaching a greater consensus on goals. Executive management is then able to decide with some degree of finality what the majority of organization goals for the coming year will be. Should significant difference exist between the input of the constituencies and that of the executive management, the board of trustees may become the final arbiter at the time the goal statements are presented to the governing body for their input and approval. The final draft is distributed to the constituencies and becomes the official list of goals for the coming year; it provides the basis for later delegation of assignments or goals to subunit managers.

The third step in implementing an MBO program requires that each subunit's purpose and how it is integrated into the whole of the organization be understood and agreed upon. Each subunit (such as academic affairs, career education, social sciences, and the English department) must justify individual purposes and understand how they serve the overall goals. A helpful technique is for the chief executive to request that each manager define in three sentences or less the purpose for the subunit's existence. In each case, the purpose statement should clearly indicate the reasons for and the functions of the unit in assisting the organization to fulfill its mission.

The following purpose statement, for example, may

60

well be typical for the academic affairs subunit: "In order to maximize each student's opportunity to learn and develop, the purpose of academic affairs is to provide in the most creative and effective manner possible the programs necessary to satisfy the educational needs of the community, including courses and programs necessary for transfer to four-year colleges or universities, courses and programs in career areas, continuing education, community services, and adequate support for these programs and the community through the Learning Resource Center." (The Learning Resource Center, a relatively new term and concept, is an expansion of the traditional library and includes its function, along with additional learning devices such as tapes, slides, films, cassettes.)

An example for the financial affairs subunit might be: "To maximize each student's opportunity to learn and develop, the purpose of financial affairs is to provide a high quality business affairs organization that operates on the basis of contemporary management concepts to provide management information, efficient physical facilities, materials, and supportive services as its contribution to achievement of the college mission."

As a fourth step, position descriptions must be available for all organizational jobs. Job descriptions provide the basis for establishing regular objectives, authority, and accountability relationships. Once the purpose of each subunit is established, supervisory individuals must be accountable for work to be accomplished by them if the subunit purpose and the organization mission are to be met. Position descriptions are needed for each individual down through the first level of supervision.

The position description is perhaps the most important building block and reference point for measurement of individual accomplishment in management by objectives. It is of paramount importance that job descriptions be contemporary and have mutual agreement of the manager and his subordinate, which can be best guaranteed by annual updating and reviewing by the manager and the subordinate.

Fifth, each subordinate must establish his major performance objectives for the coming year in measurable terms with specific deadline dates. Having reached agreement with the manager on his position description, the subordinate develops a set of individual objectives, a realistic guideline of what he plans to accomplish within the parameters of the job description. Open discussion of these objectives between supervisor and subordinate will foster the principle of involvement and commitment.

The sixth step toward implementation of an MBO system requires that the subordinate and supervisor enter into a joint review for a mutually agreed upon set of objectives. Experienced managers will agree that there is almost always a gap in what the supervisor and subordinate perceive a job to be. Odiorne (1965) claims that research accumulated from the study of individuals in business and industrial organizations reveals that a 25 percent difference exists between the way the manager views the job and the way the subordinate views the job. It is clear why both individuals must discuss their differences until agreement is reached. Each must feel commitment to the goals and to the success of that which he had a part in influencing, and the subordinate must understand that the supervisor assumes accomplishment of the objectives to be on the schedule unless the subordinate has reason to call their attentions to a potential deviation. The supervising manager, acting in the role of a coach, must emphasize the importance of reaching the goals and of seeking help before rather than after a failure.

Seventh, date schedule is agreed upon and established for the purpose of reviewing progress. At an agreed upon time interval, the supervisor and his subordinate should review progress toward objectives. They may choose to update and revise goals at this time. These scheduled review sessions provide excellent opportunities for coaching and development techniques by the supervisor and foster open and healthy communication.

Eighth, a report summarizing major accomplishments and variances between results achieved and results expected is prepared by the subordinate at the end of the year. After a series of recorded progress interviews and as a result of drawing up the accomplishment report, the subordinate communicates his level of performance to his supervisor. Through this summarization the subordinate is aware of his continuing progress because of the goal-setting and reviewing processes with which he has been involved. These processes minimize the need for constant supervision.

As the ninth step, the annual accomplishment report is discussed jointly by supervisor and subordinate. To make objective assessments, the supervisor must guard against the temptation to engage in personal observation about the individual. Assessment should be outcome-oriented and not based on personal attributes. As in the scheduled interviews throughout the year, the supervisor has excellent opportunity at this time for coaching and fostering good working relations.

The tenth step is the establishment of a new set of objectives for the next year. Through the processes of review, coaching, and development, new ideas and experiences may have emerged that may be incorporated into the goals for another year. The accumulation of knowledge that results from the close working relationship and open communication is very valuable in assessing realistic goals for the following year.

Eleventh and lastly, long-range objectives are reviewed and adjusted in accordance with the degree of achievement for the present year goals, and a new commitment is made to new objectives.

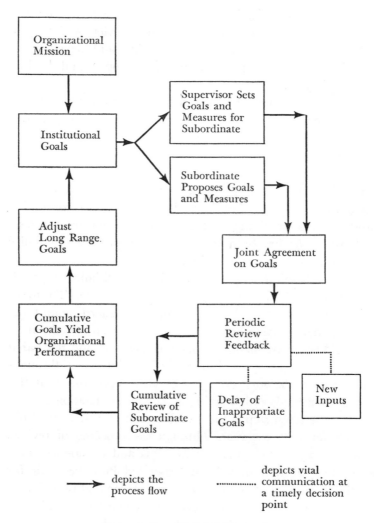

depicts the process flow   depicts vital communication at a timely decision point

FIGURE 2.   The MBO cycle.

Figure 2 delineates the relationships of these steps in the MBO cycle.

The following paragraphs summarize six major management weaknesses in higher education and the MBO approach to coping with them. The first weakness is the failure to plan and to set goals. MBO is based on planning—long-range, short-range, organization-wide and for subunits. It requires the establishment of a central purpose and function understood and agreed upon at all levels.

A second weakness is that administrative jobs are not defined by objectives. Under MBO, position descriptions are available for all jobs, and the objectives of the organization, its subunits, and its individuals are stated precisely. Third, management skills are lacking. MBO requires unusually precise attention to the job of managing, and the feedback from performance reviews serves as a basis for self-development. Although additional training in management skills is essential, the system provides a perfect stage for an administrative development program or management development vehicle.

An attempt to continue a "one-man show" operation is a fourth weakness. Under MBO, the individual manager's span of control is maximized and made more effective. The system forces delegation of authority and responsibilities. A fifth weakness is the uncertainty about who makes what decisions. Position descriptions provide the basis for authority and accountability relationships and for establishing routine objectives. Areas of accountability are further pinpointed by periodic review of the objectives. And finally, information-gathering processes are inadequate. Under MBO, the prerequisite for setting and reviewing objectives is adequate information, which is to be shared at all levels of supervision.

Chapter 6

Setting Individual Objectives

The most crucial activity in the MBO process is the setting of objectives; it is crucial because objectives are the base for determining what is to be accomplished and how well the activities have been performed. Fundamentally, there are two aspects to setting objectives: identifying and agreeing on the objectives along with an order of priorities; and writing the objectives in a usable form to be effective tools for supervisor and subordinate.

Identifying objectives requires that the manager consider his total job as it now is and to reflect on new developmental activities. It is not essential that all activities be reflected in objectives; a manager's effectiveness is partially his ability to analyze groups and concentrate his attention on those objectives that will offer the most progress, benefits, or results as determined by priority determination.

Setting Individual Objectives

In giving priority to objectives, visualize a hierarchy of three categories: first, absolutely necessary objectives determining success or failure; secondly, objectives necessary for improved performance; thirdly, objectives desirable for improved performance, objectives which could be postponed to a later date.

Because objective-setting is the most crucial and difficult part of mastering the implementation of MBO, top management must offer coaching assistance in the early stages of objective-setting. Needless to say, the setting and writing of objectives is a new approach to the work of an educational manager, who will find the process challenging. Objectives should be written in simple, straightforward statements describing results the manager expects to achieve; the objective is a communication vehicle between the supervisor and subordinate.

Four kinds of objectives have been defined by Odiorne (1968): regular objectives, problem-solving objectives, creative-developmental objectives, and personal objectives. A routine or regular objective is a repetitive, commonplace, but necessary goal characterized as being a stabilizing influence. The problem-solving objective is a performance modification that leads to correction of a deviation, discrepancy, or deficiency in a level of current performance. A developmental objective is a new and different approach that leads to improved or expanded results and promotes growth and development. A personal objective is an individual effort that leads toward the improvement of professional or managerial skills and the enhancement of career growth, promoting individual growth.

Regular, problem-solving, and developmental objectives developed properly should be challenging, measurable, specific, limited in time, realistic, well integrated into the

67

organization, and representative of a commitment between the employee and supervisor. For example, "to develop and publish the fall 1972 master schedule for adult and continuing education by July 1, 1972," is a regular objective. "To decrease the production time for the president's report from 120 to 90 days in order that distribution can commence not later than January 1, 1972," is a problem-solving objective, and "to develop and administer a morale survey for nonexempt employees prior to June 1, 1973," is a developmental objective. "To research and review ten programs or publications relating to nontraditional studies as a preliminary to recommending such a program to the president of the college," is a personal objective. Objectives developed at William Rainey Harper College, listed in the section on Implementation Procedures, are intended to be a detailed guide for objective identification in other two-year colleges.

Objectives will evolve from within the scope of a manager's job description and will surface as he carries out the functions outlined. Setting objectives for the first time may present difficulty to the manager, but he can be guided through experience and interviews with an immediate supervisor. Where the manager is positioned on the organization chart— for example, whether he is a staff member, vice president or division chairman—should noticeably affect the number and kinds of objectives he constructs for the position. The objective-writing process is often so stimulating that the routines of a job may suffer because of overdedication to it. Care must be taken to maintain proper balance. Routine objectives sometimes suffer because of the extreme challenge of problem-solving and creative-developmental goals.

The manager may find it helpful to estimate the percentage of time required to achieve each major objective or major category of objectives. Assigning weighted values to each objective facilitates arranging them in a priority order.

In the discussion of objectives, supervisor and subordinate should consider what type of job performance would warrant marginal, below average, satisfactory, above average, or meritorious rating. The individual can thus better understand what is expected on the job, although attention must be paid to the abilities and experience of each man. What might be considered outstanding performance for a new employee may be considered reasonable for a more experienced employee. It is important for the supervisor to emphasize that outstanding performance on one or two objectives will not circumvent the expectation for at least reasonable performance on all other objectives.

Objectives must be constructed in light of ability and experience of the individual, time, personnel available, resources, and authority to achieve objectives. The supervisor and the subordinate should understand that objectives may be enlarged and improved upon year after year until a certain mutually agreeable standard is reached.

Objectives will often overlap, and it is rare that an objective will not require some relationship with more than one person. In itself, there is nothing wrong with overlap; in fact, it could be an effective way of promoting teamwork between individuals or units. Involved parties must be cognizant of and agree to give the necessary effort to achieve the objective on a given time schedule.

It is ultimately the joint responsibility of the supervisor and the subordinate to determine whether objectives are realistic, in proper order of priority, and integrated into the overall objectives of the subunit and the organization. It is often helpful to ask questions. For example, do the manager and subordinate agree on the assignment of priorities? Is the time frame reasonable for the accomplishment of each objective singly and all objectives combined? If there are overlapping objectives, have other supporting parties been notified, and have they agreed to their responsibilities and the time schedule? Are the objectives too demanding of the individual or too easy? Will the objectives add to an interrelated matrix or will they be at odds with other managers and units? Can accountability for final results be clearly established? Do the objectives relate directly to the manager's job description? Is the objective clear to those who may be required to implement it? Will the result justify expenditures in time, money, and other resources to achieve it? Objectives should be quantified in terms of percentages, weights, ratios, numbers, dollars, time, or volume. Organizational morale can be measured, for example, as grievances, requests for transfer, absenteeism, turnover, complaints, or sickness. The most precise possible quantification of objectives is important for two reasons: The measures applied in a statement of objective help to define that objective, and quantified objectives can be used as the standards against which current operations are evaluated. A precisely quantified objective may make the difference between having the feeling that progress is being made and knowing exactly what progress has been made.

Nonquantifiable objectives can be set by describing a condition that will exist when the objective is reached. Another guide to measuring the intangible but critical improvement areas is to identify specific activities that should logically lead to improvement. An example of a nonquantifiable objective would be to implement an improved system of communication with students during the 1972–1973 calendar year. This objective will be achieved when an evaluation of the present system is established, a weekly bulletin for students is implemented, the adequacy of student posting areas is reviewed with representatives of clubs and the student senate, and a monthly rap session is established with differing groups of students.

Sound objectives are stated in terms of end results, are achievable in a specified time period, are specific as to the form of accomplishment, are realistic and attainable, are important to the success of both unit and organization, are stated as precisely as possible in terms of quantities, and are limited to one important commitment. They improve personal effectiveness, create commitment between the employee and his supervisor, integrate the organization, and are consistent with available or anticipated resources. Poor objectives are stated in terms of activities or processes, are not achievable in the time specified or at all, are ambiguous, are theoretical or idealistic, are of no real consequence, are too brief or indefinite, or are too long or complex. They lack requirements of improvement, involve no commitment or agreement, are outside the mission or purpose and at odds with other departments, or are too costly. Sound objectives tell what and when; poor objectives tell why and how.

After institutional objectives are defined, they must be delegated into the organization in order to achieve desired results. For example, the institutional objective "to increase the institutional average class size from twenty-four to twenty-seven students for the 1971–1972 academic year" falls within the responsibility of academic affairs and is delegated to the Dean of Academic Affairs. The dean's objective now reads: "To explore and reach agreement with each division chairman on the necessary average class size for each division in order to achieve an institutional class size of twenty-seven students during 1971–1972." The objective now breaks down to each academic division where individual division objectives are coordinated by the dean. The division objectives might be "to achieve an average class size of twenty-five students for all classes offered in the Division of Business during 1971–1972," and the divisions must achieve this balance to reach the original institutional goal.

Meaningful objectives give meaning to the organization. Whether pleasant or unpleasant, work is more tolerable, and even enjoyable, if it leads to a meaningful end (Myers, 1970). Myers maintains that factors that make objectives meaningful and energize people to achieve them are generally defined in terms of the characteristics of the objectives themselves. Objectives that have maximum motivational value; that are influenced by the objective setter; and that are visible, desirable, challenging, and attainable should lead to satisfaction of needs—both institutional and individual.

Chapter 7

Advantages of Management by Objectives

Management by objectives is designed to minimize core problems facing education and other organizations by integrating organizational objectives and individual needs, changing traditional power structures, building intergroup teamwork, adapting the institution to environmental elements, maintaining the institution's identity under constant change, and providing for constant organizational renewal.

Integrating individual needs and organizational objectives can be accomplished through understanding, involvement, and motivation. If the manager understands the organizational objectives and his role in helping to accomplish them, the need to fulfill these objectives becomes his need, and he is better able to identify with the organization. By becoming involved, as in the objective-setting process, the individual is more genuinely committed to his work, and achieving the objectives he has helped to develop really matters to him. Participation by all managers in a management system builds teamwork and unity and establishes an organization "way of life."

MBO has built-in provisions for establishing motivation toward organization objectives. Self-fulfillment, the internal satisfaction of successful accomplishment, often results precisely because measurable objectives have been planned by the individual. Objectives seem easier to achieve because they are clearly defined and understood. Feedback from performance reviews serves as a basis for self-development, increases the individual's chances for future success, and increases his satisfaction with self-improvement. MBO creates a common ground and a feeling of acceptance and security for widely different personalities. The appraisal interview offers the ideal opportunity for expression of approval and recognition by the supervisor of the subordinate's performance. The organization has a more objective (and less personality-oriented) appraisal method for management performance and thus has a better basis for assessing management compensation according to management contribution. Appraisal and coaching is done in light of performance results, not in terms of personal or professional inadequacies. Under MBO, there is a constant challenge to continually strive to meet defined objectives. The encouragement of creativity in the approach to objectives allows for greater flexibility, new ideas, inspirational thinking, and brainstorming.

MBO recognizes the need to change traditional power structures through definition of the individual's authority, through delegation, and through self-control. The manager's span of control is more clearly defined and more effective because of the objective setting, the accurate and current job descriptions, and the performance appraisal. The delegation process provides better-balanced work loads, and the supervisor becomes more keenly aware of the responsibilities each position entails. The individual and his supervisor play more equal roles with similar information and a greater area of common knowledge. Full participation by all managers of the organization builds teamwork and encourages a total-effort approach to achieving objectives. MBO reinforces the delegation process in which supervisors must delegate not only responsibility but also authority. Self-control replaces control imposed by the supervisor, and individual initiative is encouraged.

The need to build intergroup teamwork is met through communication, definition, and common objective commitment. Necessary communication upward, downward, and laterally in the organization is aided by the MBO system. Interaction between subunits is reinforced by a clear understanding of individual and organizational objectives. Common goal commitment, or the combined effort and interest to achieve objectives, helps individuals who work in teams to keep their conflicts and disputes in the open where they can be readily dealt with and resolved. Because achieving the defined objectives is what counts, there is less emphasis on personality or on personal characteristics. Competition between groups or specialists is replaced by team spirit of cooperation.

The need to adapt the organization to environmental elements is accommodated by MBO because all components—internal and external—relative to the organization are involved in and committed to the successful functioning of the organization; there is a strong liaison between the organization and its environment. Increased awareness of significant environmental trends and changes by the organization facilitates adaptation.

The organization's need to maintain a clear identity under constant change is met by clearly stated objectives that serve as a compass to point effort in the right direction and to offer standards for measuring progress. Planned, periodic reviews afford opportunities for assessment and coaching and allow adjustment of objectives before major problems develop. Emergency projects are not likely to divert the completion of organizational priorities because of the flexibility and stability inherent in the system. Because objectives are integrated and understood at all levels, a stable continuity is maintained even when managers change.

The vital need for constant organizational renewal is accomplished through communication, organizational self-analysis, and control. Information about organizational status, new developments, and prospects for the future is shared at all levels of supervision. Objectives are reviewed and, if necessary, revised and updated on a regular basis. End-of-the-year examination of accomplishment requires organizational self-analysis and highlights areas in need of revitalization. Position descriptions and accountabilities are continually reviewed, adjusted, and updated to meet changing conditions. These reviews, this introspection, and this adjustment make it possible to attend to change before major problems develop.

MBO is not a cure-all, an all-purpose system, a management speedup system, or a gimmick for increasing managerial production. As with any system of management, MBO has its limitations and potential pitfalls. Odiorne (1965) identifies four major limitations. The system does not appraise and identify potential; therefore, the system places the burden on a supervisor to assess lack of results in light of his responsibility for coaching and development. The system presumes the man and his boss will together establish suitable standards that will serve the company well. It implies that the boss understands his limitations and will refrain from playing God. In action, the system stresses results and does not provide methods of achieving them.

Advantages of Management by Objectives

Additional cautions should be observed in implementing MBO. First, it is not an easy system to implement. Full implementation requires three to five years; once in effect, the system requires hard work and a strong commitment. There must be a willingness to invest a tremendous amount of energy in the MBO system before results are seen. The benefits are great, but they do not come easily. Secondly, the process must be taught, and the teaching must be continually reinforced through management development before a manager becomes proficient in utilizing the principles of the system. Thirdly, the system places a burden on the supervisor in that he must be able to assess actual results rather than activities that seem to indicate results. (A significant factor here is that there is a 25 percent difference in how the boss sees the job as opposed to his subordinate's view of the job.) Fourth, some managers, despite extensive training, are unable to learn to manage with objectives. They fail either to define objectives in proper quantitative terms or to conduct effective appraisal interviews to reinforce the principles of participative management. (Educators have a tendency to describe rather than quantify, which sometimes presents a problem in objective setting and evaluation.) Fifth, overlapping objectives are difficult to set, attain, and evaluate. Managers can therefore rationalize the inability to meet goals.

There are several potential pitfalls of the system. Employees can become frustrated if they are led to feel that each year increasingly higher goals will be demanded. Overemphasis on the achievement of objectives, to the exclusion of more routine and administrative work, can undermine managerial effectiveness. Also, employees must not be overwhelmed by a sea of paper in the MBO process. Thirdly, the quality of objectives deteriorates at each level if strong coaching and development are not stressed. Fourth, coaching should not

77

always be left until the time of the annual or quarterly review. If, for example, there is to be an administrative change, coaching should be done at that time.

MBO is a complex system and when hastily applied can create problems in the organization or fail to produce results. The problems are generally caused by weaknesses in the managers and are not inherent in the system. The system most commonly fails because of poor monitoring, ignored feedback, lack of commitment, uninvolved managers, too little coaching and assistance, objectives "handed" to subordinates, lack of planning to reach objectives, overemphasized or mechanical appraisal processes, overemphasis on objectives rather than perspective on the whole system, omission of periodic reviews, inability to delegate, too much paper work, stifled creative goals, and hasty implemention.

Because of the complexity and subtleties of MBO and the challenge for new managerial organizations, it is of paramount importance that monitoring, feedback, and resource consultation be provided on a regular basis. These efforts will serve to reinforce and motivate or to locate areas of difficulty. During the monitoring and feedback process it is important that top management pay particular attention to the negative comments or problem areas in order that corrective action may be implemented as rapidly as possible.

Business and industrial organizations that have successfully implemented MBO agree that benefits of MBO are the facilitation of change, the identification of developmental needs, the production of objective reward criteria, the facilitation of a coordinated effort, the reinforcement of managerial effectiveness, and the enhancement of the job of managing.

MBO benefits the individual supervisor by providing a good coaching framework, strengthening weak appraisal methodology, strengthening the supervisor-subordinate relationship, and motivating subordinates. Perhaps the most important benefits accrue to the subordinate; his authorities and responsibilities are clarified, he is aware that he will be measured by performance and results rather than personal characteristics, he knows what is expected of him, and he experiences increased job satisfaction.

In order to assess the value of the MBO system, monitoring and feedback from educational managers who have been involved in the process are particularly helpful. Information gained from a survey administered one year after MBO had officially been in effect at Harper College indicated the reactions of thirty-seven managers to the MBO system. Top management's failure to respond to the weaknesses listed could have doomed the system to failure; third party consultation was introduced, and additional time was set aside for managers to exchange opinions, discuss results of feedback, and offer suggestions for improvement. Another portion of the first-year evaluation survey solicited information about the manager to determine whether MBO was having any adverse effects on his adjustment within his job or the organization.

A more comprehensive follow-up of the MBO process was introduced after four years of experience with the system in the same educational environment. Care was taken to construct a survey instrument that would not only serve in the initiating organization, but would assist in the identification of strengths and weaknesses of MBO implementation by other organizations. The response as measured by the survey was predominantly positive with many more strengths identified than weaknesses. The MBO evaluation questionnaire utilized at William Rainey Harper College with tabulated results is listed in the section on Implementation Procedures. Sizable minority of those tested felt that MBO moved away from humanness; administrators found difficulty in writing objectives; a sizable minority felt that the appraisal process was overemphasized and communication needed to be improved;

there was too much blame and avoidance behavior as opposed to problem solving behavior; some felt that MBO induced more anxiety into the organization than is necessary; some felt the need for job enrichment and improvement in reaching agreement on priorities, evaluation of output, decision-making, and other utilization of facilities; supervisors had most control of the rating process, although managers felt they had the same input into the process.

Organizations that have had experience with MBO conclude that under a committed management the system has great potential for developing more skillful and productive managers and improving organization efficiency. Appropriate preparation for and thoroughness of implementation minimize weaknesses and maximize strengths of MBO in later stages. Actual implementation demands high amounts of effort, time, energy, and patience and can be an exhausting but very rewarding experience. A paramount prerequisite to implementation of MBO is a high degree of commitment by management. Implementation is not an end in itself but demands highly important follow-up activities.

Chapter 8

Appraising the Organization and Its Management

The development of more precise measurement and evaluation requires clearer definition of educational aims and individual purposes of the two-year college. Goal definition provides a more realistic base for directly measuring outcomes in terms of desired educational objectives. By its nature MBO aims the appraisal process toward evaluation on the basis of outcome by placing the traditional form-and-structure concept in proper perspective within a more encompassing and accurate evaluation pattern. Form and structure embody important elements but consist generally of concrete or tangible tools of the organization—for example, the length of a board member's term of office or the size of the library collection. Essential to survival are the activities performed by, with, to, or through these tools—managing, goal-seeking, developing, creating, communicating, and motivating. Essential to evaluating the success of the organization is a clear understanding of the product to be produced and a close scrutiny of the many activities that go on prior to a guaranteed product.

Two-year college administrators and faculty must assume the major responsibility for assessing the effectiveness of their organizations with the aid of qualified external auditors. An institutional self-study preceding an on-site audit by an auditing team should continue to be a most effective approach to gauging performance. In this activity, institutional personnel (administration, faculty, and students) give careful consideration to defining the task of the institution and to assessing the ways in which it is endeavoring to accomplish its purposes. The self-study should describe the institution, indicating its strengths and weaknesses; set forth its plans for remedying these weaknesses; and project plans for future development. Emphasis on gauging institutional performance should be given to: stated institutional mission; target area and population to be served, with complete and accurate identification of the population needs of the service area; base data describing the characteristics of entering students; evaluation of student progress at the end of each course program or achievement year level; evaluation of graduates; evidence of accomplishment of other institutional objectives (research, community service); institutional dynamics (governance and committee structure, administrative organization, student organizations); and description and analysis of decision-making mechanisms and long-range goals of the future.

Ways of gauging an institution's performance have been suggested by authors Beckhard (1969) and Gardner (1965a). Beckhard claims:

82

Appraising the Organization and Its Management

An effective organization is one in which: (a) The total organization, the significant subparts, and individuals, manage their work against goals and plans for achievement of these goals. (b) Form follows function (the problem or task or project determines how the human resources are organized). (c) Decisions are made by and near the sources of information regardless of where these sources are located on the organization chart. (d) The reward system is such that managers and supervisors are rewarded (and punished) comparably for: short-term profit or production performance, growth and development of their subordinates, creating a viable working group. (e) Communication laterally and vertically is relatively undistorted. People are generally open and confronting. They share all the relevant facts including feelings. (f) There is a minimum amount of inappropriate win/lose activities between individuals and groups. Constant effort exists at all levels to treat conflict and conflict situations as problems subject to problem-solving methods. (g) There is high "conflict" (clash of ideas) about tasks and projects, and relatively little energy spent in clashing over interpersonal difficulties because they have been generally worked through. (h) The organization and its parts see themselves as interacting with each other and with a larger environment. The organization is an "open system." (i) There is a shared value, and management strategy to support it, of trying to help each person (or unit) in the organization maintain his (or its) integrity and uniqueness in an interdependent environment. (j) The organization and its members operate in an "action-research" way. General practice is to build in feedback mechanisms so that individuals and groups can learn from their own experience.

On the other hand, Gardner claims an effective organization is one that is self-renewing and follows the following rules: "The first rule is that the organization must have an effective program for the recruitement and development of talent. The second rule for the organization capable of continuous renewal is that it must be a hospitable environment for the individual. The third rule is that the organization must have built-in provisions for self-criticism. The fourth rule is that there must be fluidity in the internal structure. The fifth rule is that the organization must have some means of combating the process by which men become prisoners of their procedures."

Although the authors identify the effective organization in different ways, both suggest that assessment of the internal activities of the organization rather than the form and structure is the key to effectiveness.

Managers within the organization structure are responsible for a wide range of activities and processes—managerial systems, planning processes, accountabilities. Because the manner in which these are carried out significantly influences the health of the organization, it is essential to scrutinize closely managerial effectiveness. The most important ingredient for assuring that the institution accomplishes its mission is leadership. The educational manager is accountable for making things happen and must expect to be measured by the results he achieves. Minimal requirements for managing managers are effective identification, recruitment, and selection procedures; contemporary, written job descriptions; an organized development program; a formally organized salary administration program with incentives; and a commitment to a promotion ladder system coupled with a strong policy of promotion from within yet tempered with sufficient external recruitment to eliminate complacency from inside managers. Assuming that minimal requirements for the managing managers have been met, a formal evaluation program for educational managers is an additional necessary ingredient.

Appraising the Organization and Its Management

Inherent in some appraisal approaches is the reasoning that if people are the most important part of an organization, evaluation should be made on personal characteristics—initiative, common sense, ambition, tact, sincerity, and drive. In addition to the fact that this approach ascribes a numerical value to unquantifiable qualities, there are other pitfalls. Who decides which traits are to be rated? Can there be agreement on a definition of each one? Are some traits assets in some jobs and liabilities in others? Should all traits have the same relative value? Can prejudice by the rater be adequately overcome? Even when appraisal forms center on performance itself, the appraiser has questions. How well does this employee overcome problems? Does this employee display any special qualities when working with his peers? How does this employee perform under pressure? Typical answers read: "This employee shows a lot of common sense in overcoming problems. He is very cooperative with his peers. He works calmly under pressure." For all practical purposes, trait measurement has run its course in business and industry and hopefully in education as well.

The results are obviously inadequate. Beneficially, many organizations have turned to a goal-oriented appraisal, which focuses on measurable accomplishment. At any given moment an employee should be working at something that is measurable and that contributes to an organization's major objectives. Goals describe why a job exists in the first place: We don't have an employee to operate a machine; we have him there to produce so many units, meet certain specifications, and do so at a certain cost by a definite time. An effective performance appraisal system as part of MBO should have certain objectives. The first is the improvement of performance in the job assigned. The appraisal procedures should not dwell on the past but should move to a future action plan based on what has been learned from the past. The second objective is the development of people in two ways: providing the organization with people qualified to step into higher positions as they become open and serving to help individuals who wish to acquire knowledge and abilities to become eligible for higher jobs. The third objective is to provide answers to the questions: "How am I doing?" "How should I be doing?" and "Where should I go from here?"

The appraisal program is fundamentally a five-step process. First the individual discusses his job description with his supervisor, and they agree on the content of his job and on the relative importance of his major duties in the things he is paid to do and is accountable for. Next the individual establishes performance objectives for the majority of his responsibilities for specific periods of time. These performance objectives should be specific, measurable, limited in time, and realistic, as described in detail in Chapter Five. In step three the individual meets with his supervisor to discuss and reach agreement on his performance objectives for the specific period(s) of time. It is essential to reach mutual agreement on the performance objectives, the results desired, and the level of achievement to be accomplished. As the fourth step, at least three appraisal interviews should be established as check points for evaluation of progress. Fifth, supervisor and subordinate meet on the specific dates scheduled for an appraisal interview, and a record should be made of the exchange.

The appraisal interview is used to assess the progress and productivity of each administrator in carrying out the goals and objectives he and his supervisor have agreed upon. In keeping with the spirit of the MBO system, anxiety-producing aspects at the appraisal experience should be minimized for both the supervisor and for his professional; both individuals are emotionally involved in the review because each has agreed to the original objectives.

Basic to a successful appraisal interview is a definitive

job description for which goal-setting has been correlative. The supervisor must be aware of the major elements of the subordinate's job and should spend at least thirty to forty-five minutes in preparation for the interview. During the preparation period a plan for the interview should be developed, past performance and interview data should be reviewed, and the supervisor should refresh himself on the goals and objectives to be discussed. A poorly prepared supervisor is certain to produce anxieties for himself or the subordinate.

The most productive role for a sensitive supervisor is to listen attentively while the subordinate evaluates his progress in carrying out each goal, objective, or major element of his job description. The supervisor should be careful not to interrupt but should look for the most natural opportunity to probe or clarify the subordinate's verbalizations. Careful probing or clarification should produce agreements on areas to be improved or adjustments needed for goal completion.

Goals not met or off schedule should be adjusted or a plan devised to put them back on schedule. In all cases both individuals should agree to each condition, and the appropriate note would be made by the supervisor for the summary essential to the closing of a good interview.

Most significant to the interview will be the degree to which a supervisor is able to create a nonthreatening atmosphere and a respectful exchange of opinions. Within the interview and as subtly as possible, near the end of the evaluation, the professional should be provided the opportunity to respond to questions which it is the supervisor's obligation to ask. The degree to which a supervisor is able to listen attentively and quietly to the professional's response to each question he poses will be significant to the quality of the relationship that will continue between the two. The questions should include: Are your duties and responsibilities adequately defined? Do you find your work sufficient and challenging? Do you feel your work and ability are appreciated? Do you feel you get the backing and support you need? Are you informed and consulted when you should be? Do you feel you have access to me to talk things over freely? Do you have the authority and opportunity to exercise initiative? Do you feel your opportunities are adequate? What could I or others do to help you do a better job? What kind of place, in general, do you feel this is to work? What other things that you like or dislike about your job would you like to tell me?

While performance appraisal usually calls for an evaluation of the employee's work on an annual or semiannual basis, good timing is more important than an efficient but inflexible schedule. Employee goals seldom have exactly a twelve-month or six-month deadline; some will take one month to achieve, others three months or a year or more. Unquestionably, any evaluation that praises accomplishment of a task is more beneficial at the time of accomplishment than some months later. If performance appraisal is to be an effective part of healthy managerial programs, it must include well timed feedback to let the manager know how he is doing.

Reaching the goal is not the sole measure of success; some goals will be surpassed and some never even approached. The person who sets meager targets and always hits them is certainly of no more value to the organization than the person who sets unreachably high goals, falls short consistently, but in doing so makes substantial contributions to the organization or improvements over his past work. The important elements are the results achieved by the total process of establishing objectives, striving to attain them, and analyzing what intervenes between planned and actual performance. When the final assessment is made, the individual should be evaluated on his ability to set targets as well as his ability to attain them. In checking results, the supervisor should emphasize success and build on successful accomplishments and should assume the responsibilities for coaching and development for unsuccessful accomplishments observed.

Tosi, Rizzo, and Carroll (1970) suggest that performance evaluations should rarely be based on the achievement of an objective or on the sheer number accomplished. They suggest consideration be given to: quantitative aspects (was cost reduced 5 percent as planned?); qualitative aspects (have good relations been established with department X?) deadline considerations (was the deadline met or beaten?); proper allocation of time to objectives; type or difficulty of objectives; creativity in overcoming obstacles; additional objectives suggested or undertaken; efficient use of resources; use of good management practices in accomplishing objectives (cost reduction, delegation, good planning); and coordinative and cooperative behavior (avoidance of inducing conflict, unethical practices).

After the performance appraisal interview has been completed and a thorough discussion and evaluation has taken place between supervisor and subordinate, the organization should be prepared to reward those who have contributed to the achievement of organizational objectives and to withhold reward from those who have not. The reward system might be based upon five major performance categories: marginal performance, below average performance, satisfactory performance, above average performance, and meritorious-to-superior performance. Each performance category considers the degree of attention to the following items: percent of objectives completed; fulfillment of job description requirements; quality and quantity of work; efficient use of resources; organization and planning ability; leadership and good management practices; and cooperative and coordinative relationships with other personnel. Detailed performance categories and the performance appraisal form utilized at William Rainey Harper College are listed in the section on Implementation Procedures, p. 146.

If the supervisor has been successful in his appraisal interviews and other on-the-spot coaching and development activities, each subordinate should be well aware of his performance during the year and should be able to classify himself into one of the preestablished performance categories. The assignment of a monetary reward to each category assures every manager that equity will prevail and that the reward is based on prevailing competitive salaries and availability of funds in the institution.

The performance and appraisal process is advantageous for organizational development for many reasons. The subordinate knows in advance the basis on which he will be judged because he and his supervisor have earlier agreed on his responsibilities. Because the process is based upon a supervisor-subordinate relationship, it helps to strengthen this relationship. The process has a self-correcting, personal growth characteristic that assists people in setting goals that are challenging and attainable, and the process provides a method of spotting individual development needs, thus setting the stage for a total managerial development program within the organization. Also, the performance appraisal system highlights a total managerial approach that allows the individual manager to better understand his personal contribution to the organization as he strives to meet institutional goals.

Chapter 9

Planning Process

Most essential to the effectiveness of the Management by Objectives system is long-range planning, a dynamic strategy that forces management to contemplate the future and what management can and should do about it. Planning well done means goals well begun and will save countless hours of effort in striving to reach those goals. The terms *long-range* or *short-range* imply that planning has the boundaries of time spans, and this assumption is true. The purpose of planning, however, is to make decisions today knowing that stages of futurity will be within time spans of tomorrow. The effectiveness of planning depends upon a clear assessment of present conditions (where are we) and insight into future trends (what will probably happen) in light of our desired goals (where we wish to go). For example, a long-range planning goal for a two-year community college might be to double the number of seminars offered by the division of community services in four years. A short-range planning goal, made within the framework of the long-range goal might be to increase the number of seminars offered by the division of community services by ten during the current fiscal year.

Short-range objectives that have not been made within the framework of long-range objectives run the risk of slowing down the forward motion of an organization and consequently creating inefficiency in reaching the objectives. Similarly, the long-range plan cannot be alive, vibrant, realistic except in account with today's decision-making process; without this relationship many long-range plans end up in desk drawers. For example, a short-range planning goal which is in conflict with a long-range planning goal might be to shift the academic calendar of College X during the current year in order to conform with four-year colleges to which College X sends the majority of its students. Whereas, the long-range plan stipulated that College X at the end of three years enroll at least 80 percent of the mid-year high school graduates from the three supporting high schools in the district. Long- and short-range plans differ not only in time frame but also in commitment. In the short-range plan, commitments are firmer and more easily expressed in concrete terms. As the time frame lengthens, this specific quantitative aspect becomes more vague and qualitative, and when one looks a decade ahead the quantitative factors all but disappear. Short-range objectives can be viewed as a tactical plan that directs an operation in the immediate future. Long-range objectives, on the other hand, constitute a strategical plan that outlines steps that should be taken on the basis of assumptions regarding the institution's future environment. Taken a step further, the long-range objectives constitute a conceptual plan that delves deeper into research and development needs and sets controls for the strategical plan.

In order to plan adequately we must understand that a long-range plan is not a slick, leatherbound document but an ongoing process of goal-seeking through controlled means. The plan document loses its effectiveness the moment this activity ceases. Any document produced during the process does not contain absolutes that lock planners into a particular course. Rather, the document is based on assumptions that must be continually reviewed, modified, and updated. Long-range planning is not crystal-ball-gazing. Planner and author Peter F. Drucker points out (in Ewing, 1972, p. 5) that long-range plans deal not with future decisions, but the futurity of present decisions. The question now facing the planner is, what do we have to do today to be ready for an uncertain tomorrow? Not, what will happen in the future? Planning in its simplest sense is a control system exerted before an action is taken. A good long-range plan should include objectives, assumptions, expectations, alternative courses of action, decision points, impacts, and an assessment of results. Objectives set a course of action and provide a base against which to measure results. Assumptions are necessary because many factors about the future are unknown. Expectations provide psychic energy in setting the direction of the planning strategy. Alternative courses of action provide flexibility. Decision points are those points at which a specific step of the plan is ignited into action. Impact takes into account what effort is required, by whom the activating is done, and what the effects are on people and areas of the organization. Assessment of results provides feedback on the intended or unintended effects.

Appropriate planning provides college leaders with the tools necessary to control rather than react to change. It enables college managers to avoid making crisis decisions, which are rarely long-term solutions anyway but merely stopgaps inclined to collapse under the pressure of the next emergency. Planning also enables them to lead with a management of efficiency rather than a management of fear. Planning provides managers with a deeper understanding of their organization. Hidden strengths and weaknesses are revealed, unrecognized facets of the operation are uncovered, and, by the time the compilation of a master plan is completed, the management knows its institution far better than before. The plan document benefits both the lay community and the college constituencies. For the public, the list of objectives serves as a measuring stick to judge an institution's performance. For the college community, it serves as a guide that orients the present to what has happened in the past and to future events, thus giving perspective and direction.

The typical long-range plan in higher education deals primarily with enrollment projections and physical spaces (buildings). Effective long-range planning for the two-year college should include projected enrollment data, educational strategies, staffing projections, financial projections, and physical space needs and projections. A plan should have well interrelated goals and priorities with interim steps and decision points clearly visible. All of this information should be bound into a master document accessible to all staff and personnel for their guidance purposes. To carry planning through successfully to the point of a written document, there must initially be an energizer or a strong leader who guides a planning team (or a group selected to collaborate in this effort). The energizer, often the institution's chief executive or his planning officer, is responsible not only for directing a centralized planning effort but also for implementing the planning objectives defined. Initially, what happens depends primarily on the chief executive. Until he recognizes the need for major change and assumes or delegates the role of energizer, nothing much is likely to happen. Because the plan eventually developed must be one with which he can live, he must of necessity participate actively in its preparation.

If a chief executive fails to recognize the importance of planning or seems unable to apply the process to his organization, the institution's board of trustees has the responsibility to ask questions that force the process. A chief executive's inability to lead the long-range planning process should be sufficient grounds for release. Questions that an effective board of trustees should ask of its chief administrator are: Are the top managers giving only lip service to the need for long-range planning and carrying on their business as usual? Is the long-range planning process being represented only by form (document) rather than by substance (action)? Does the long-range plan have practical significance for influencing the thinking and decision-making of organizational constituencies? Are the plans practical and realistic, identifying organizational problems as well as opportunities? Are there valid projections of the future environment in which the organization will find itself, or are projections simply based on present and past conditions? Does the board see evidence of managerial intuition for calculated risk-taking? Is the management so tied to traditions or the institution's founding objectives or so eager for retirement that it fails to implement (or actively resists) a long-range plan?

A sincere commitment to long-range planning by college management manifests itself in the methodology and approach to the planning process. Under persuasive managerial leadership, all entire resources of the institution are involved in the setting of goals and directions for the institution, and a resourceful leader will welcome faculty as a source of additional input. It is important that faculty, administrators, classified staff, and students show themselves to be capable and cooperative in this productive process, minimizing adversary relationships and demonstrating the rapid progress that can be made when professional resources are cohesively organized into a common good. The institution's basic identity is that of a community college; it is necessary to bring meaning to the word *community* by involving the community in appropriate aspects of the college's long-range planning (for example,

95

through the use of advisory committees and cooperation with local municipal governments.)

Once a commitment to planning is made, the chief executive's first action must be delegation of responsibility for the process. If the institution is small, he may remain heavily involved as the prime energizer. If the institution is larger, the process may be delegated to a full-time planning officer. In either case the key to planning success is sincere involvement by representative resources of the institution and its supporting community. After delegating, if necessary, the chief executive must still recognize his responsibility to assist in getting the program under way. An appointed selection committee might be composed of the college president, a board member, a faculty member, and a student. The purpose of the committee is to screen and interview all applicants for membership on the planning committee; the applicants should be advised of the time required for and the nature of this project in order that they too be highly committed. The final selections might include five faculty, four administrators, two students, and two classified staff.

Members of the planning team should be people who are respected by their peers and, more importantly, who have trust and respect for each other as well as for the chief executive. Their contribution capabilities can be measured by their creativity, dedication, and ability to think with open minds and in broad perspective. To promote enthusiasm for the planning project, the chief executive should give membership a sense of honor and importance. Participation in planning should become a privilege in the eyes of the college community. It should not be considered extra duty but a special project for which participants are highly select; they should be granted released time and necessary resources to perform this vital service.

Once the manpower is assembled, the actual planning

can begin. There is no formula for the planning process. Each institution has its own unique situation and must find an approach that best suits its needs. However, general guidelines can be applied to most projects. They are: analysis of present situation (competition, capabilities, opportunities); establishment of future objectives (assumptions, goals); formulation of methods needed to implement objectives (programs, projects, policies, procedures); scheduling of target dates for objectives (priorities, schedules); leadership delegation; and cost analysis and cost effectiveness.

The responsibility that the chief executive entrusts to the planning committee might be explained as follows. Through the involvement of individual or representative groups of faculty, administrators, classified staff, and students, the planning committee will explore and develop alternative plans by: reviewing the objectives of the college for adequacy and agreement as to appropriateness for the future; delineating as specifically as possible the service area and population the college may be expected to serve; identifying the type and number of students, adults, and community agencies the college should expect to serve; delineating as nearly as possible the scope of programs and services the college should expect to provide in order to carry out its mission as a comprehensive community college; identifying the curricular changes, instructional strategies, and innovations that must be initiated to provide the most relevant programs for student and community needs; suggesting a plan of orderly expansion of the staff and the physical environment of the college to efficiently provide anticipated services; and developing a statement of financial requirements (capital and operational) and potential sources of revenue for carrying out the long-range plan. The committee will then file a progress report with the president on scheduled interval dates, complete the long-range planning activities and file a final report to the president by a given deadline, and stand ready to present the final report in open session to the president and board of trustees by a given date.

During its first meetings, the committee should develop a decision matrix listing plan objectives and projections along with criteria for evaluation. Suggestions for the matrix should be solicited from all segments of the institution. A sample matrix that has been successfully used at Harper College is included in the section on Implementation Procedures (p. 148)'.

Collection of background data will occupy a great deal of time. Surveys can be used as major information collecting media; questionnaires should be sent to students, faculty, administrators, district residents, and a group of similar colleges. To provide financial background, the committee must analyze the cost of proposed changes and the revenue available to implement these changes. Regularly scheduled and announced hearings should be held to obtain firsthand feedback from faculty and students and to answer questions. Interviews should be conducted with selected community leaders and other resource people. Helpful study material should include the state master plan and Carnegie Commission reports such as *The More Effective Use of Resources, Institutional Aid, New Students and New Places, The Open Door Colleges, Quality and Equality, Less Time, More Options, A Chance to Learn, The Fourth Revolution: Instructional Technology in Higher Education,* and *Reform on Campus.*

After the collection of data, ideas, and feedback, the long period of review and deliberation begins. Specific blocks of time must be set aside to accommodate this important step. Action agendas must be constructed. The first draft of the long-range plan should ensue from this process and should be sent to administrators, faculty, students, and other key people. Their suggestions should result in the production of a second draft, the basis for an interim report to the president. If the president feels this draft is sufficiently complete, an interim report and feedback session should be planned with the board of trustees. At this meeting it could be expected that the committee explore new alternatives in specific areas; that the committee provide more back-up data; and that a blue-ribbon citizens' committee be appointed to review the plan before it again comes to the board.

As a result, the committee should produce a new draft in preparation for a board-appointed citizens' committee. This committee should be broadly representative of the community, highly visible, and with low political profile. The selection, for example, might include a corporate director of planning, corporation president, bank president, hospital director, volunteer director, insurance agent, community planning commission member, attorney, management consultant, pastor, and so on. The committee responsibilities as presented by the board of trustees might include an overall review of the long-range plan of the college for the purposes of developing community understanding, support, and acceptance, and judging the comprehensiveness of the plan. The board of trustees should give the advisory committee initiation and completion dates for its deliberations as well as a deadline for the submission of a report with recommendations. Of course, the board should provide facilities, requested resources, and the necessary back-up staff to help the committee carry out its functions efficiently.

Through the help of the college president the citizens' committee should schedule meetings to reap full or at least greatest attendance. The drafted plan and other pertinent back-up material should be forwarded to committee members well in advance of their first meeting. At this first meeting, the citizens' committee chairman should review the committee's charge and take sufficient time to set the guidelines for committee deliberations. A plan of action should outline those areas that are appropriately the lay committee's responsibility and those that are the professional staff's responsibility for de-

LEWIS AND CLARK COLLEGE LIBRARY
PORTLAND, OREGON 97219

liberation and decision-making. On very specialized subjects, the citizens' committee could wisely request the appointment of special committees to assume assignments demanding additional information, attention, and discussion. The citizens' committee recommendations should be incorporated into a new draft of the long-range plan to be submitted to the board of trustees. A joint meeting of the citizens' committee and the board should be scheduled for the purpose of clarifying, if necessary, any of the committee recommendations. Upon completion of this assignment, the citizens' committee has served its purpose and may be dissolved.

A final draft of the plan should be prepared for final deliberation by the long-range planning committee, the chief executive, and the board of trustees. The plan should provide recommendations for a ten-year timetable and cite specific and ongoing target dates for various activities to be undertaken. All target dates based on assumptions must be reviewed and updated as necessary. In effect, the plan states: This is where we stand now. This is what may happen in the future. These are the studies and activities we need to initiate now, next year, and within the next five years. These are the costs we can expect each year from now until ten years from now. These are the ways we can meet these costs.

Recognizing that documentation does not complete the planning process, the institution's management should establish the long-range planning committee as a permanent unit of the institution. The director of planning and development should be the permanent chairman; other members may be selected for two-year terms on a rotating basis.

As a follow-up to meetings during the academic year, the planning committee should meet during each summer to review progress on the long-range plan to that date; to review results of feasibility studies assigned and completed during the previous year; to review five-year plans assigned to and made

100

by suborganizational units during the previous year; to revise and add new recommendations to the long-range plan on the basis of progress and results; and to recommend that new feasibility studies be begun when appropriate.

If an institution's leaders and constituencies are truly committed to planning they are not satisfied with simply turning out a plan document. They see the necessity for perpetual introspection and modification to keep the plan vital and currently relevant. The elements outlined above do not constitute the completion of the planning process but rather are the beginning of a recurring cycle that, if well maintained, can render the institution very responsive to change—a desirable course of development and productivity.

Chapter 10

Effective Salary
Administration

An equitable salary program depends on valid job classifica-
tions, periodic salary review of competitive levels, performance
appraisals, and effective salary planning. The lack of these
interrelated and essential primary elements frequently leaves
the two-year college with numerous unresolved wage and salary
problems. Higher education faculty and administrative salaries
have escalated rapidly in the past decade and are approaching
parity with other professional salaries in business and industry.
However, according to the Carnegie Commission (June,
1972), faculty salaries will probably increase less rapidly than
wages and salaries generally in the 1970s. During the 1960s,
salaries went up with the cost of living plus 3 or 4 percent, but
in the 1970s it is estimated that faculty salaries are more likely
to rise no more than 1 or 2 percent beyond the cost of living—
and possibly even less. If faculty salaries are approaching parity

with other sectors, it will behoove college management to build systems to ensure continued equity and control.

With the spread of collective bargaining in higher education, good salary practices are even more essential. Ineffective practices or inadequacies in wage and salary structures will serve as a catalyst for grievances and make the collective bargaining process more difficult for management. In a number of post-secondary institutions, predominantly the two-year colleges, ineffective planning and inexperienced educational administrators and boards have led to the annual renegotiation of the salary schedule, which negates its potential function as a tool for control in business and industry.

Higher education must give recognition and reward for differing levels of performance in the same job and give less consideration to time in the position and educational preparedness. There is a need for better job definition and classification as well as more sophisticated salary survey data on a greater and wider number of institutions. The most recent salary study (1972) conducted by the College and University Personnel Association included only 277 out of an estimated 1100 two-year institutions and only 961 institutions out of a estimated total of 2555 collegiate institutions in the United States.

Salary problems in higher education are not surprising in view of the source from which the majority of educational administrators are recruited. Even though an educational administrator might choose to pursue a doctorate in administration, it is highly unlikely that his program will include instruction or exposure to wage and salary principles. Bolton and Genck (1971, pp. 283, 287–288) made the following observation on top management staff functions in colleges and universities:

The personnel function is typically focused almost entirely on clerical and operating personnel matters. A fully professional approach is seldom evident at these levels, where large bud-gets . . . demand sound plans for employment, classification, and compensation administration. More significant is the absence of competent personnel staff support for administrative and faculty personnel matters, especially for recruitment, com-pensation, and manpower planning. . . . Administration ser-vices for all university personnel should also be provided at the top management level. Major and long-range benefits to uni-versities should result from a professional and comprehensive personnel function. Since university personnel activities are typically far less developed than in industry, the acquisition of qualified people to develop this function should be feasible. Responsibilities of a strengthened and expanded personnel function should include: (a) providing manpower planning and staff recruiting services for both administrative and faculty personnel, (b) directing personnel services for clerical and labor personnel, including employment, allocation, and salary administration, (c) maintaining records and administering benefits programs for all personnel.

The task of wage and salary administration is a broad and complex one. Wage and salary programs generally reflect four dominant goals: equity, competitive position, control of labor costs, and motivational efforts. More specifically, wage and salary administration programs purport to control wages and salaries in the organization to ensure that expenditures are serving their proper function and are neither too low nor too high; to maintain consistencies throughout the organization by establishing standard wages for similar jobs and job classifica-tions (crucial to complying with affirmative action legislation designed to eliminate discrimination of any kind); to adjust wages and salaries with changes in labor markets; to pay more money for more complex and more responsible jobs; making promotion a more desirable goal for motivated employees; to recognize the principle of merit (compensating the individual employees according to their proficiency within their respective job classifications) to provide more incentive to perform better; to improve the ability of supervisors and executives to deal with wage questions raised by employees; and to provide rational methods of adjusting wages.

Through an effective wage and salary administration program, other desirable objectives can be obtained within an organization—more equitable compensation to encourage and satisfy the ambitions of employees, more acceptable evaluation of specialized services, a reduction of wage exploitation, and encouragement of capable management.

To establish an effective wage and salary program, several factors must be considered. First, average wage or salary levels must be set to secure and keep a productive work force. Major considerations in these deliberations are the public, competitors, and perhaps a union, as well as salaries paid for comparable work in nearby communities or similar businesses.

Some plan or wage and salary structure must also be established so that more difficult and more responsible jobs are compensated at a higher level. A logical hierarchy of jobs can establish pay as relative to job status within the hierarchy.

Thirdly, individual wage determination requires deliberations as to whether all employees doing the same job should receive the same wage or salary. If not, management should decide how to differentiate the compensation of similarly employed individuals as well as how an individual is to obtain a raise in pay.

Another factor, the payment method, determines whether to pay employees on a time basis (hours per week or a monthly salary) or on some type of incentive system. Various other pay plans and the balancing of financial and nonfinancial rewards are options.

The factor of indirect compensation includes insurance premiums, holidays, length of service bonuses, study grants, sick leaves, and so on.

Another consideration is compensation of exempt employees. (The Fair Labor Standards Act of 1938 defines nonexempt employees. The nonexempt employee is covered by the act unless work, responsibility, and pay do not meet the specific criteria defined by the act, which establishes a minimum hourly wage and maximum hourly work week, after which overtime pay is necessary.) The exempt employee is not covered by the act. Although compensation objectives for managerial and professional employees do not differ significantly from those for other employees, the compensation solutions do. A main difference is the greater work commitment expected from the exempt group; thus compensation arrangements that carry strong motivation implications are required.

The problem of control is a factor that concerns the ability of the organization to pay, keeping salaries within the ranges set for jobs and keeping the general level of wage and salary in tune with labor markets where employees are able to witness adjustments in individual wages and salaries on a consistent and regular basis. Control is the central problem of wage and salary administration for the employer.

The major steps to the development of a comprehensive salary administration program for both exempt and nonexempt personnel are development of position descriptions, position analysis and job evaluation resulting in classification, and establishment of compensation schedules. Position analysis has certain major purposes: to describe major duties and responsibilities of the job or position; to define organizational relationships of each component and aid in preventing overlap of duplication of work effort while assuring that all necessary duties and accountabilities are assigned; to aid in establishing a common understanding between employee and superior as to what is expected and required of the incumbent; to provide for delegation of authority, fixing of responsibility, and defining of accountabilities; to provide the basis for position evaluation; and to serve as the basis for appraising performance. Performance appraisal of all personnel in an organization is an essential ingredient to organizational effectiveness. Although all personnel (exempt and nonexempt) may be covered by similar statements of purpose, it is imperative that each group (executive-managerial, professional-faculty, clerical-technical) have an individually designed appraisal system.

No new position should be filled until an analysis or description has been written, approved, and evaluated. This principle is particularly important when individuals are hired from the outside, since starting salaries must be based on approved and evaluated statements. Position analyses and job description questionnaires for newly created positions require approval of the preparing manager and his immediate superior before submission to personnel for evaluation.

Position evaluation is the responsibility of management and is coordinated by the personnel office. Exempt (managerial) positions, as defined in position analyses, are evaluated by a committee of managers utilizing a guide chart developed by the personnel office. Each position is individually evaluated in terms of know-how, or the sum total of every kind of skill, however acquired, required for acceptable performance; problem-solving, or original self-starting thinking necessary for the position for analyzing, evaluating, creating, reasoning, arriving at, and making conclusions; and accountability, or the responsibility for action and the consequences thereof. It is the measured effect of the position on end results. The result of position evaluation is the basis for relating positions in terms of their value or relative worth in accomplishing organizational or institutional goals.

Exempt (executive) position evaluations are based on variables very similar to those for managerial positions. The main factors are basic responsibilities or major duties and the scope of responsibilities or size of the organization that the executive leads or to which he provides staff services.

A number of approaches have been utilized to determine the value of executive positions over the years, but today two basic approaches are used by the majority of businesses and industries. The first is the point-factor method discussed in exempt (managerial) evaluation. The second is the marketplace method, which allows the marketplace to arbitrate the question of a position's worth. Ultimately, a position is worth what the market says it is worth. Six basic steps are involved in the marketplace method: selecting a number of benchmark positions (positions whose mix of duties and responsibilities is common to many organizations); selecting a number of competitive organizations; surveying benchmark positions for current pay rates; designing a compensation structure to cover the position being evaluated; placing benchmark positions in the compensation structure in accordance with their market worth; and incorporating all remaining positions into the structure on the basis of a comparison of their duties and responsibilities with those of the benchmark position now known and graded.

Nonexempt jobs, as defined in job description questionnaires, are evaluated by a guideline method of job evaluation. Key jobs throughout the organization are placed in salary grades on the basis of comprehensive salary survey data that determine what other employers are paying for directly comparable jobs. Those jobs for which valid salary comparisons cannot be made are then evaluated (using a job description questionnaire such as that included in the section on Implementation Procedures) by comparing them with key jobs already graded. In cases where consensus of opinion cannot be gained as to the value of a particular job through this comparison method the job evaluation plan (see Implementation Procedures) is employed as a check on the evaluators' job-comparison judgment.

Position evaluation of all jobs is made entirely on position worth as opposed to person worth. In other words, no consideration is given to the person in the position during evaluation; it is the position that is being evaluated and not the incumbent.

Upon completion of the job description and position analysis and upon their formal acceptance by management, each supervisor has the responsibility for determining when a new or revised write-up is required. If one is needed, the appropriate manager or supervisor sees that it is properly prepared and approved. Approval indicates that all statements are correct and that the incumbent will be held accountable. The incumbent should always receive a copy of the approved form.

The equating of total evaluation points and grades with dollar ranges is properly the responsibility of the personnel staff and must be in compliance with management's previously stated objectives. *Salary structure* is the term used to denote the total of all salaries paid by the organization in order of position worth; it is a composite picture of all salary ranges by classification. Its purpose is to assure that positions within the organization are in proper relationship to one another. The competitive position of the organization is reviewed annually, and changes are made when deemed appropriate by top management.

One of the greatest problems in wage and salary administration in the two-year college is the professional (teaching faculty) compensation program. The predominant derivation of two-year college faculty salary schedules in the United States is from secondary teaching schedules. The most prevalent approaches to salary schedules for teaching faculty are the step-column schedule and/or an indexed schedule reflecting increases as a result of years of experience or education hours accumulated from the bachelor's degree through the doctorate or its equivalent. The assumption is that additional experience and more graduate hours make the faculty much more valuable or more effective. These systems may have mathematical logic but relate minimally to performance based on evaluative techniques. Automatic salary increases based on experience or additional graduate hours constitute a system that, when coupled with tenure, commits an organization to indefinite employment of the individual without sufficient guarantee of the quality of his output.

Faculty salary schedules should contain minimum and maximum figures for specific classifications based on market data. Raises should be based on inflationary factors, evaluation, and the ability of the organization to pay. Should the organization wish to offer reward for additional graduate hours, a one-time grant should be offered as reimbursement. Should collective bargaining affect an organization, the schedule should not be subject to annual renegotiation, although increments of pay may be. It is the responsibility of management to determine the frequency and necessity of schedule readjustment. When collective bargaining is employed by faculty, the board and administration must of necessity engage in productivity bargaining if management is seriously concerned about cost control. Productivity bargaining by educational management should demand more or better learning at the same cost; the same or better learning at less cost; or significantly greater learning at a greater cost. Lahti (1973, p.

37) discusses fifteen ways of increasing staff productivity, many of which could be introduced into the collective bargaining process.

The challenge to management is to create an environment that motivates people to perform at a high level and fosters organizational growth. A key factor in this challenge is a reward system that offers not only base wages and salaries but nonfinancial incentives and benefits, performance appraisals, and self-fulfillment for the employee.

Chapter 11

Making It Happen

To retain the managerial habits and practices of the past will only extend and intensify the confidence and financial crises that assault higher education today. The best practices of managers are ahead of us. They are coming into existence, are beginning to reap significant success, and are molding habits and shaping patterns of action that are attuned to a society whose most common challenge is change. Traditional efforts cannot be kept reverently in orbit when in fact they fail to deal adequately with change. The rapid emergence of management as a new profession in the educational ranks will have great impact.

The self-developed leader is rapidly disappearing if not already gone from progressive organizations. Additionally, trained two-year college managers in a predominantly theoretical environment have not and will not meet the needs of the comprehensive community college. The two-year college needs leaders with personal experience supplemented by a thorough knowledge of theoretical research. The secret of effective leadership is proficiency in applying managerial skills through practice and knowing what to apply at the appropriate time.

Effective management orients itself toward individual human behavior and the environment that best affords the oportunity for self-realization in consort with the most purposeful contribution to the organization. Weighing heavily in the effectiveness of management is the individual manager's potential, his style of management, his philosophy, and his capacity for growth and development. It is not enough that the manager have honesty, purpose, dedication, and other virtues; he must be able to extend these qualities to those individuals for whom he is responsible. Poor performance is improvable; part of the mission in building effective management is the development of effective people. People, then, become a dynamic force whose competence determines the success of an organization. Ineffective managers, or those unable to deal prudently with people, are often the primary cause of ineffective organizations.

The challenge of increasing managerial competence at the workplace is a new frontier for the two-year college, one that may bridge the gap for potential managers who are properly "pedigreed and papered" but lack practical know-how. A foundation for building managerial competence is a development program tailored to the specific needs of the organization and recognizing the importance of wisely allocating resources among many competing priorities. Clear thinking, rational analysis, and an appropriate blend of management skills are extremely important conditions for organizational success if not survival.

Colleges, like all human-oriented institutions, are organized to achieve a purpose. In the case of colleges, objectives have been so broad and lofty they cannot satisfy the public with a reasonable objective-measurement system. Unlimited objectives combined with highly constrained resources force all organizations to face the question of efficiency or cost-effectiveness and the need for comprehensive planning or organization development systems. In the interest of survival, colleges will have to state their objectives more clearly and concisely and then implement better indicators of effectiveness, outputs, or value-added concepts in order to satisfy the public as to how well they are achieving the objectives for which they were initially called into existence. Value added suggests an enrichment as the result of operating within a collegiate environment which would allow a person to function more effectively in society.

Management by objectives is a system that can aid in better objective setting, measurement of outputs, short- and long-range planning, and other vital functions of effective management. Management effectiveness throughout the organization is greatly influenced by the effectiveness of the top managers or the governing body of trustees and their administrative teammates. A majority of a chief executive's work and his subordinate managers' work is accomplished by and through others. The board and administration, an inseparable team, are of necessity intertwined by virtue of the fact that the board's most important responsibility is the selection of the chief executive officer, the approval of his team, and the general surveillance and evaluation of their effectiveness. In this age of accountability, the performance of an organization is as closely allied to the performance of the board as to the performance of the chief executive officer and his leadership team. The most effective organizations will have performance standards and methods of measuring effectiveness for both board and administration as well as for other constituents of the organization. Individuals at all levels of the community college organization are accountable.

Making It Happen

The community college has many challenges. In order to justify its place in the spectrum of postsecondary education it must demonstrate its effectiveness by having good knowledge of each student's condition at the time of admission. With its open-door policy, the community college is committed to admitting but selectively placing a student population with an achievement level lower (on the average) than the typical four-year college or university or postsecondary norm group. The challenge of accepting, placing by career objectives, and demonstrating a credible contribution to the education of both transfer and nontransfer students at a defensible unit cost lies with the community college managers and faculties.

In contrast to the university that has evolved on the basis of individual, departmental, or college entrepreneurship, the two-year college has been created for the purpose of meeting unfulfilled needs of the society—the identification of community and service area needs related more specifically to individual needs and problems. The two-year college must be able to concentrate on its smaller service area and to relate the solutions to the larger society.

The purposes for which the two-year colleges have been called into existence are: the two-year transfer function (from high school through upper division higher education); the counseling and development function accompanying the open-door concept (assessing where an individual is in development, acknowledging and integrating a realistic goal for the potential assessed); the adult and continuing education function (retraining, updating knowledge or skills, more effective use of leisure time); the beginning of a career ladder for the individual who might temporarily stop off at a point after weeks, months, or one or two years of education; and the community service function (institutes, cultural enrichment, stimulation, and coordination of needed outside services for its community).

The question for the two-year college is not what to do;

115

the main problems are sorting out priorities and applying proper methodology within the resources available. Managerial leadership of the two-year college must acknowledge its role, persuade or choose people committed to this mission, and then proceed to demonstrate outputs or value-added concepts inside of this acknowledged mission.

Implementation Procedures

The following procedures are offered to those readers who desire additional detailed information on understanding and implementing the system discussed in this text. The data and format are intended only as a guide. The reader is urged to give them further refinement for his own particular situation and implementation. The author may be contacted for further information and explanation of these materials.

MBO Objectives

Goals and Objectives, 1972–1973,
Vice President of Academic Affairs

I. Regular Objectives
   A. Maintain a teaching faculty staff plan which includes class size, part-time to full-time ratios, student contacts per week, minimum class size, and minimum enrollments

per week. This objective will be considered achieved when:

1. A class size of twenty-six (average) is achieved at midterm of each semester.
2. At least 8 percent of all credit hours between 8:00 A.M. and 5:00 P.M. are taught by part-time instructors.
3. The student contacts per week of each faculty member range from 255 to 750 depending upon discipline and program and guidelines of each area of the college.
4. Enrollments in new career programs (first or second year of operation) would be twenty-five or more students in their freshman year and fifteen or more in their sophomore year.

B. Appropriate articulation efforts are made to assure that courses designed to transfer are being accepted by public institutions and universities in the state. This objective will be considered achieved when:

1. Ninety percent of all courses to transfer are accepted as regular offerings within the first two years of public colleges and universities in the state to which 60 percent of students transfer.
2. Follow-up studies and visitations are planned for fall by May 1. Evaluations and results will be completed by January 1 of the next academic year.

II. Problem-Solving Objective

A. Enlarge the cooperative education experience for students in career programs. This objective will be considered achieved when:

1. A review of all career programs which could have cooperative experiences as a part of instructional effort is made and summarized by November 1.
2. A plan is developed and adopted for cooperative experiences to be included in at least 10 percent of

118

all career programs of the college. This plan is to be adopted by January 1.

3. Appropriate staffing and work study experience arrangements have been made by May 1 for all programs.
4. An avenue for evaluation has been developed and is ready for implementation by fall.

III. Developmental Objectives

A. Explore the Instructional Development Program, which would provide the opportunity for individual faculty programs and self development. This objective will be considered achieved when:

1. A college model for Instructional Development has been studied by selected members of the teaching faculty and coordinator of the program. A model will be explored, developed, and adopted by March 15.
2. At least three faculty members have completed at least two units of instruction within the framework of the adopted model. These units of instruction will be completed by May 15.
3. An evaluation is made of the Instructional Development Program and a plan developed by June 15 for continuation and enlarged participation.

B. Evening and Continuing Education Services will expand for the next academic year. This objective will be considered achieved when:

1. An increase of at least 10 percent has been achieved for the overall offerings in Continuing Education. This objective will be considered achieved when at least ten additional workshops and seminars are successfully completed.
2. At least thirty industrial and business seminars and workshops are successfully completed by May 1.
3. At least twenty division and graduate courses are stimulated and coordinated through the college by surrounding colleges and universities.

119

4. At least twenty-five additional special courses related to hobby and leisure time activities have been successfully completed by May 1.

5. Evaluation of all the above offerings are rated by participants as at least 75 percent satisfactory.

Goals and Objectives, 1972–1973,
Vice President of Business Affairs

I. Regular Objectives

A. Nonacademic Policy and Procedure Manual revised and approved by September 30, 1972. This objective will be considered achieved when:
1. The manual is approved by the Executive Council.
2. The manual is adopted by the Board of Trustees.

B. Long-Range Facilities Manual revised and approved by January 1, 1973. This objective will be considered achieved when the manual is approved by the Executive Council.

C. Completion of at least three performance interviews during the year with each manager reporting to the vice president of business affairs. This objective will be considered achieved when completed performance interview forms are on file.

II. Problem-Solving Objective

A. Develop a plan with timetable for the completion of working drawings for Phase IIb and the remaining parts of the Campus Master Plan. This objective will be considered achieved when a recommendation is made to the Executive Council by November 15, 1972.

III. Developmental Objectives:

A. Develop improved budget systems to improve accountability and a conversion to a form of PPBS. This objective will be considered achieved when a proposal is presented to the Executive Council by December 1, 1972.

B. Develop a budget CPM that provides for timely decisions. This objective will be considered achieved when a completed budget CPM is presented to the Executive Council by December 1, 1972.

Goals and Objectives, 1972–1973, Vice President of Student Affairs

I. Regular Objectives

A. The in-service program is continued, focusing on the professional growth of the student affairs staff. This objective will be considered achieved when:
  1. A weekly staff meeting is held for the dean and directors.
  2. A monthly meeting is held for the entire student affairs staff.
  3. Phychiatric consultation in concert with the counseling staff is provided at least once a month to discuss current psychological problems of students.
  4. Appropriate professional reading material is circulated regularly to the staff.
  5. One retreat for the total staff and one retreat for the dean and directors is held to discuss goals, objectives, and results of the external audit.
  6. The staff participates in appropriate professional meetings on a state and national level.

B. The job descriptions for managers in the student affairs area are reviewed and updated. This objective will be considered achieved when all job descriptions are reviewed, updated, and rewritten, if necessary, by July 1, 1972.

C. The latest court cases are studied and the college is kept apprised of the latest changes and clarification of the law as it applies to students and student conduct. This objective will be considered achieved when:
  1. The College Law Digest is read regularly.
  2. A file is kept on recent court cases and rulings.

121

3. College officials are notified and kept apprised of rulings that affect their areas.
4. All correspondence and communication pertaining to student affairs with the board attorney are coordinated through the vice president's office.

II. Problem-Solving Objectives

A. Provide complete access to student data for the divisional counselors and the admissions office. This objective will be considered achieved when:
   1. Microfilm readers are installed in the counseling offices as well as in the admissions and central counseling offices.
   2. The records are updated seven times during the academic year.
   3. Students are randomly sampled by the student provost and indicate that their academic advising and registration were enhanced as a result of the counselors having accurate data on their status.

B. Review and evaluate the community counseling services provided to non-Harper students. This objective will be considered achieved when:
   1. A monthly financial report is submited to the vice president of student affairs.
   2. A quarterly report is submitted by the director indicating the comprehensiveness of services provided.
   3. The community counseling center has no more than a 25 percent deficit at the end of the 1972 fiscal year.
   4. Recommendations are provided by the director of the Community Counseling Center relative to the future governance and management of the auxiliary operation.

III. Developmental Objectives

A. Develop and implement a method of describing accountability for all student personnel services. This objective will be considered achieved when:

Implementation Procedures

1. The student affairs managers design and implement an internal audit including beneficial, professional, and performance ratings.
2. Three educators familiar with the community college field are selected and brought to campus prior to February 15, 1973, for a minimum of two days for purposes of an intensive evaluation of the services rendered students through student affairs.
3. Guidelines are provided for the external auditors, including a thorough cost analysis.
4. Written reports (internal and external) are submitted to the president which thoroughly discuss the pros and cons of the services provided as well as recommendations for change.

B. Continue the development of a student leadership program that could serve as a model for other colleges. This objective will be considered achieved when:

1. Nationally recognized experts are contracted to present seminars to student leaders on topics related to effective leadership.
2. Follow-up seminars conducted by student affairs and instructional staff are held at a minimum of four times per year.
3. The leadership programs are fiscally supported by the Student Senate budget and evaluated by the students for their value and success.

MBO Evaluation Questionnaire

This questionnaire is an evaluation instrument for MBO and was developed for the purpose of identifying the strengths and weaknesses of the MBO system after four years of operation at a two-year college.

It was constructed so that any organization using MBO could conduct this same evaluation. Listed in summary totals are the responses of the forty participating administrators.

Innovative College Management

I. MBO general

1. Rate the degree to which you are personally committed to MBO. Check one.

16	A.	Very committed
21	B.	Committed
2	C.	Gone along
1	D.	Indifferent
—	E.	Opposed to it

2. Which most accurately describes your perception of the MBO system in your institution? Check those which are appropriate.

2	A.	It causes the participants to be bogged down in a mire of paperwork.
2	B.	It sounds good in theory but has no effect on members of the organization.
27	C.	The system helps members plan better.
20	D.	The process aids employees in developing themselves to improve their performance.
7	E.	MBO generates a lot of anxiety among the participants.
18	F.	MBO provides objective criteria by which employees can be fairly evaluated.
1	G.	The system calls for too many coaching, developing or counseling conferences which waste valuable time.
2	H.	It requires too many meetings to make decisions.
1	I.	Other (specify) _____

3. What effect does MBO have on the organization? Check one.

2	A.	It causes the organization to be very humanistic and strongly oriented toward people.

Implementation Procedures

17	B. It produces a tendency in the organization toward more humaness and concern for people.
1	C. It has no effect.
13	D. It produces a tendency toward less humaness and concern for people.
1	E. It causes the organization to be much less humanistic and oriented toward people.
6	F. I have no idea what effect MBO produces.

4. The following lists a critics consensus about educational management. Mark (M) beside the alternative in which MBO has been most effective in correcting at your institution and (L) beside the alternative in which MBO has been least effective in correcting.

M	L	
11	4	A. Placid leadership
16	4	B. Lacking in management skills and systems
13	5	C. Poor long range planning process
28	3	D. Lack of clearly defined goals
4	10	E. Inefficient utilization of facilities
8	5	F. Ineffective budgeting practices—the more available money, the higher the costs
7	10	G. Inefficient decision making
4	19	H. Lack of agreement about priorities among constituents of the organization
6	14	I. Insufficient evaluation of the quality of output

II. Objective formulation

1. When you write your own objectives, how satisfied are you with the results? Check those that apply.

18	A. My objectives pretty accurately reflect my total job responsibilities.

   4   B. I find creative goals are stifled as a result of the objective writing process.

   14   C. My finished objectives don't adequately reflect the importance of my routine duties.

   18   D. I find some of my goals are difficult to quantify and therefore aren't adequately reflected in my finished objectives.

   4   E. I am dissatisfied with my finished objectives in other ways. (specify)_____

2. To what degree do your finished objectives relate to the institutional goals? Check one.

   24   A. They are closely related.

   13   B. They are somewhat related.

   2   C. They are not related.

   1   D. I have no idea what the institutional goals are.

3. What has been your experience with coaching to help you write your objectives? Check one.

   1   A. I have no need for coaching.

   27   B. I have received the coaching I needed from my supervisor.

   5   C. I have received the coaching I needed from other persons.

   4   D. I have received the coaching I needed from the literature.

   4   E. I needed help in writing the objectives but I have not received adequate coaching as yet.

4. How are your objectives set? Check one.

   —   A. My supervisor determines my objectives for the coming year.

126

Implementation Procedures

<table>
<tr><td>14</td><td>B. An intermediate condition between A. and C.</td></tr>
<tr><td>19</td><td>C. There is an interaction process whereby my supervisor and myself mutually determine and agree upon my objectives.</td></tr>
<tr><td>6</td><td>D. An intermediate condition between C and E.</td></tr>
<tr><td>1</td><td>E. I set my own objectives and my supervisor mechanically approves.</td></tr>
</table>

5. How familiar are you with your immediate superior's objectives? Check one.

<table>
<tr><td>4</td><td>A. We go over them together.</td></tr>
<tr><td>17</td><td>B. I am familiar enough so that my objectives mesh with his.</td></tr>
<tr><td>12</td><td>C. I have a fairly good idea of what his objectives are.</td></tr>
<tr><td>3</td><td>D. I have a vague idea of what his objectives are.</td></tr>
<tr><td>4</td><td>E. I have no idea what his objectives are.</td></tr>
</table>

III. Implementing objectives

1. What has been your experience with coaching to help you implement your objectives? Check those appropriate.

<table>
<tr><td>3</td><td>A. I have no need for coaching.</td></tr>
<tr><td>27</td><td>B. I have received the coaching I needed from my supervisor.</td></tr>
<tr><td>9</td><td>C. I have received the coaching I needed from other persons.</td></tr>
<tr><td>2</td><td>D. I have received the coaching I needed from the literature.</td></tr>
</table>

_____3_____   E. I needed help in implementing my objectives but I have not received adequate coaching as yet.

2. Once your objectives are determined, who determines how these objectives will be achieved? Check one.

_____16_____   A. I solely determine the implementation process (within budget restrictions).

_____22_____   B. My supervisor provides some general guidelines for implementing my objectives.

_____2_____   C. My supervisor maintains close control on how I implement my objectives.

IV. Appraisal process

1. How many times in the last year have you and your supervisor gone through the appraisal process or reviewed your objectives? Check one.

_____—_____   A. Never
_____21_____   B. Once
_____12_____   C. Twice
_____6_____   D. Three times
_____1_____   E. Four times

2. What was the effect of the review process with regard to your objectives? Check those appropriate.

_____3_____   A. No effect—it was a very mechanical process.

_____9_____   B. I discovered some unrealistic objectives and was allowed to change them accordingly.

_____27_____   C. Because of unforeseen events, the review allowed some objectives to be revised or deleted.

Implementation Procedures

18	D. Because of new demands some new objectives were added.
3	E. Other effects (specify)_____

3. What was the effect of the appraisal process with regard to implementation of your objectives? Check those appropriate.

7	A. No effect, I had things well under control.
4	B. No effect, it was a mechanical process.
25	C. I discovered some areas where more emphasis needs to be placed.
4	D. I discovered areas in which I need more coaching and made the necessary arrangements to receive this coaching.
2	E. I discovered areas in which I need more coaching but I have no idea where to go from here.

4. Do you feel the appraisal process is overemphasized at your organization? Check one.

4	A. Definitely yes
10	B. To some extent
5	C. No opinion
10	D. It is doubtful
11	E. Definitely no

5. In the appraisal process how do you feel you are rated? Check one.

4	A. I am rated on my personality traits.
24	B. I am rated by the results I achieve.
3	C. My supervisor simply rates everyone in the middle.

—	D. My supervisor simply rates everyone at the top.
11	E. Other (specify) _____

6. In the appraisal process, how is your rating achieved? Check one.

11	A. My supervisor tells me my rating.
18	B. An intermediate condition between A and C.
8	C. We mutually agree on my rating.
—	D. An intermediate condition between C and E.
—	E. I determine the rating I will receive.
3	F. Other

7. How fairly do you feel you are rated during the appraisal process? Check one.

5	A. I am underrated. I know other people in the organization doing no better job than I am who receive better ratings.
26	B. I feel I am fairly rated.
—	C. I feel I am overrated compared to other people I know in the organization.
9	D. No opinion.

8. What is your reaction when you receive negative feedback in the appraisal process? Check one.

—	A. I react negatively branding the criticism as unfair and defending myself to my superior.
1	B. I react negatively to the feedback given but I keep my feelings to myself.
13	C. I have an immediate negative gut reaction but later I objectively evaluate the criticism. If I feel the feedback was fair I

130

Implementation Procedures

	try to correct my behavior and if I feel it was unfair I ignore the criticism.
16	D. Same as C above except if I feel the criticism was unfair I let my superior know about it.
1	E. I react negatively but I put on a good show trying to convince my superior that I have responded positively to his criticism.
9	F. I react positively to almost all feedback, negative or positive.

9. What kind of problems do you encounter arriving at a rating during the appraisal process? Check one.

18	A. No particular problems
3	B. It is difficult to measure the results called for in the objectives.
1	C. It is difficult to reach agreement on whether or not the objective has been achieved.
15	D. It is difficult to summarize results achieved on all the objectives in one rating.
3	E. Other (specify)_____

V. Description of organization

1. Describe your perception of the communications climate in your organization. Check all those which are appropriate.

8	A. Many people in the organization say one thing but mean something else.
18	B. There are very few individuals in the organization with whom I feel free to discuss my real feelings concerning job related activities.
12	C. When people talk to each other they are usually pretty honest with one another.

<u> 11 </u>   D. People in the organization don't talk with one another enough.

<u> 15 </u>   E. Communication breakdowns in the organization occur not by design but because of neglect and ineffectiveness.

<u> 9 </u>   F. There is generally an adequate free flow of communication within the organization.

2. When a problem occurs how do you perceive most individuals in the organization reacting? Check those appropriate.

<u> 15 </u>   A. Search for someone to blame

<u> 22 </u>   B. Take immediate steps to protect themselves from the blame

<u> 21 </u>   C. Engage in a problem-solving process

<u> 6 </u>   D. Avoid facing the problem

<u> — </u>   E. Other (specify)_____

3. Can creative change occur readily within the organization? Check one.

<u> 9 </u>   A. Yes, whenever change can be justified.

<u> 13 </u>   B. Intermediate step between A and C.

<u> 12 </u>   C. Only after much effort and a long period of time.

<u> 6 </u>   D. Only after a monumental effort.

<u> — </u>   E. It is hopeless.

<u> — </u>   F. No opinion.

4. Do you feel you have the ability to effect major change in the organization? Check one.

<u> 4 </u>   A. I can have a great deal of influence.

<u> 22 </u>   B. I can have some influence.

<u> 11 </u>   C. At best I would have a slight influence.

Implementation Procedures

    2   D. I feel completely powerless.

    —   E. No opinion.

5. Describe the promotion and development potential in your organization as far as you are concerned, and check one.

    1   A. I am at as high a level of responsibility as I ever want to be.

    7   B. There are good opportunities for me to be promoted.

   10   C. While there is a very slim opportunity for me to be promoted as such, my present job and responsibilities could be greatly expanded.

   11   D. If I am ever to advance or develop any further in my profession I will probably have to move elsewhere.

   12   E. While there is a very slim opportunity for me to be promoted as such, I feel I am being developed professionally in the organization.

6. Where is the organization's greatest emphasis? Check one.

    3   A. It glorifies the past.

  1.5   B. It is most concerned about today.

 24.5   C. It looks to the future.

    1   D. It vacillates.

    4   E. No opinion.

    3   F. Other (specify)_____

_____

VI. Perception of supervisor

1. Generally do you find your supervisor supportive of the following aspects of the organization? Check those appropriate.

133

31	A. The organization in general
32	B. MBO system
30	C. Individual development
28	D. Institution-wide goals
26	E. His subordinates
19	F. His professional association

2. Do you feel your superior is a more effective manager as a result of MBO? Check one.

14	A. Definitely yes
12	B. Maybe
2	C. I doubt it
1	D. Definitely not
—	E. It has made him less effective
11	F. It is hard to judge

3. To what extent is your supervisor engaged in planning? Check one.

1	A. If he is I am not aware of it.
2	B. The planning that he has engaged in is too narrow and inadequate.
17	C. The planning that he has engaged in seems to be adequate. I was simply informed what these plans were.
20	D. Not only is his planning adequate but I was involved in the process.

4. How would you describe your supervisor? Check one.

5	A. Reactive (on the defensive)
3	B. Inconsistent
12	C. Proactive (on the offensive)
—	D. Inactive
3	E. Sensitive
16	F. Sensitive and proactive
2	G. Other (describe)

134

Implementation Procedures

5. How has MBO affected the relationship between you and your supervisor? Check one.

8	A. It has had no effect.
19	B. It has led both of us to a better understanding of each other's areas of responsibility.
9	C. It has led both of us to a better understanding of my area of responsibility.
4	D. It has affected our relationship in another way (specify)

6. When you have performed a significant task unsatisfactorily, how does your supervisor handle the situation? How would you like him to handle the situation? Check one in each column.

How he actually handles situation	How you would prefer he handle the situation	
24	34	A. He calls me in immediately and informs me of my unsatisfactory behavior.
11	2	B. He lets me know about my unsatisfactory performance by a series of indirect cues.
2	—	C. He says nothing in person but notes the behavior on my performance records.
2	—	D. He waits until the behavior becomes intolerable and then he tries to change my behavior or my job and responsibilities.
5	2	E. He tells me about my unsatisfactory performance at the next appraisal interview.

135

7. When you have performed a minor task unsatisfactorily, how does your supervisor handle the situation? How would you like him to handle the situation? Check one in each column.

How he actually handles situation	How you would prefer he handle the situation	
8	18	A. He calls me in immediately and informs me of my unsatisfactory behavior.
21	12	B. He lets me know about my unsatisfactory performance by a series of indirect cues.
2	—	C. He says nothing in person but notes the behavior on my performance records.
1	—	D. He waits until the behavior becomes intolerable and then he tries to change my job and responsibilities.
8	6	E. He tells me about my unsatisfactory performance at the next appraisal interview.
2	2	F. Other (describe)_____

VII. Description of job and self

1. How has your satisfaction with the job changed in the last year? Check one.

11	A. My satisfaction with the job is much higher this year than it was a year ago.
7	B. Intermediate step between A and C
10	C. My satisfaction level is unchanged.
3	D. Intermediate step between C and E

136

Implementation Procedures

3	E. My satisfaction with the job is much lower this year than it was a year ago.
6	F. It is hard to judge.

2. How has your effectiveness to perform your job changed in the last year? Check one.

13	A. My effectiveness on the job is much greater this year than it was a year ago.
18	B. Intermediate step between A and C
2	C. My effectiveness on the job is unchanged.
1	D. Intermediate step between C and E
1	E. My effectiveness on the job is much lower this year than it was a year ago.
5	F. It is hard to judge.

3. How would you describe your present job? Check one.

2	A. It challenges me beyond my ability and leaves me frustrated.
19	B. It challenges me so I am constantly increasing my achievement level.
4	C. I can handle it without any sweat.
1	D. It is so unchallenging I am bored.
14	E. It challenges me but at the same time I would like some job enrichment.
—	F. Other (describe)_____

4. How would you describe yourself? Check one.

1	A. Reactive (on the defensive)
4	B. Inconsistent
14	C. Proactive (on the offensive)
—	D. Inactive
3	E. Sensitive
17	F. Sensitive and proactive
1	G. Other (describe)_____

5. When someone under you has performed a significant project unsatisfactorily, how do you handle the situation? Check one.

____37____ A. I call them in immediately and inform them of their unsatisfactory behavior.

____2____ B. I let the person know about his unsatisfactory performance by a series of indirect cues

____1____ C. I say nothing to the person but note the behavior in his performance records.

____—____ D. I wait until the behavior becomes intolerable and then I try to change his job and responsibilities.

____—____ E. I tell them about their unsatisfactory performance at the next appraisal interview.

____—____ F. Other (describe)_____

6. When someone under you has performed a minor task unsatisfactorily, how do you handle the situation? Check one.

____12____ A. I call them in immediately and inform them of their unsatisfactory behavior.

____17____ B. I let the person know about his unsatisfactory performance by a series of indirect cues

____1____ C. I say nothing to the person but note the behavior in his performance records.

____1____ D. I wait until the behavior becomes intolerable and then I try to change his behavior or I try to change his job and responsibilities.

138

Implementation Procedures

9	E. I tell them about their unsatisfactory performance at the next appraisal interview.
1	F. Other (describe)_____

Summary of First-Year Evaluation of an MBO System*

Describe How MBO Affects Your Job	*List The Strengths of MBO*	*List The Weaknesses of MBO*
Helps me plan and keep on target. Helps me understand how my goals fit into the total institutional plan. Helps one manage more effectively. Provides stimulation for personal development. Better able to delegate and relate to subordinates. Allows one to evaluate one's progress. Evaluate others more objectively.	Measured by agreed upon objectives. Helps one plan and keep on target. Brings about understanding of relationships between goals set throughout the organization. Exposes new theories of management. I am more accountable; I can measure my output. More alert to innovative ideas.	Lack of authority to carry out objectives. Susceptible to being used punitively. Setting objectives is time consuming. Tends to promote rigidity and narrowness in plans. Frustrating experience—cannot quantify educational results. Too industrial—in style. If goals do not work bottlenecks result. No follow through. Achievement of objectives should not be the only measure. Routine responsibilities.

* Based on thirty-seven manager responses.

Innovative College Management

Administrative Performance Categories

I. *Marginal Performance*

   A. Has achieved 65 percent or less of the objectives of his position for the year, as prioritized and agreed upon with his supervisor.

   B. Frequently, and with serious implications, does not fulfill the requirements of his job description, the key areas of which are normally included under "regular" or "routine" objectives.

   C. Frequently, and with serious implications, does not produce a quality and quantity of work which include thoroughness, accuracy, and creativity required to meet minimum standards of the position, and within appropriate deadlines.

   D. Frequently, and with serious implications, does not manage his work area with efficient use of area and institutional resources.

   E. Frequently, and with serious implications, does not organize and plan for his work to meet minimum requirements and objectives of the position.

   F. Frequently, and with serious implications, does not exercise leadership, proper use of authority, and good management practices in developing and supervising subordinates, delegation and use of controls, decision making, and communications.

   G. Frequently, and with serious implications, does not exhibit coordinative and cooperative behavior in a positive manner with other college personnel in carrying out the college's mission, institutional goals, and position goals.

II. *Below Average Performance*

   A. Has achieved 65–75 percent of the objectives of his position for the year, as prioritized and agreed upon with his supervisor.

140

B. In general, and with less serious implications than the marginal performer, does not fulfill the requirements of his job description, the key areas of which are normally included under "regular" or "routine" objectives.

C. In general, and with less serious implications than the marginal performer, does not produce a quality and quantity of work which include thoroughness, accuracy, and creativity required to meet minimum standards of the position, and within appropriate deadlines.

D. In general, and with less serious implications than the marginal performer, does not manage his work area with efficient use of area and institutional resources.

E. In general, and with less serious implications than the marginal performer, does not organize and plan for his work to meet minimum requirements and objectives of the position.

F. In general, and with less serious implications than the marginal performer, does not exercise proper use of authority, leadership and good management practices in developing and supervising subordinates, delegation and use of controls, decision making, and communications.

G. In general, and with less serious implications than the marginal performer, does not exhibit coordinative and cooperative behavior in a positive manner with other college personnel in carrying out the college's mission, institutional goals, and position goals.

III. *Satisfactory Performance*

A. Has achieved 75–85 percent of the objectives of his position for the year, as prioritized and agreed upon with his supervisor.

B. Fulfills the key areas of his job description which are normally included under "regular" or "routine" objectives, but does not fulfill enough of the duties to meet the total requirements of the position.

C. Produces a quality and quantity of work with some reasonable degree of thoroughness, accuracy, and creativity, but not more than average or what is required to meet minimum standards of the position, and within appropriate deadlines.

D. Manages his work area with some reasonable degree of consideration for efficient use of area and institutional resources.

E. Manages his work with some reasonable degree of organization and planning but only to the extent of meeting minimum or average requirements and objectives of the position.

F. Exercises leadership, proper use of authority, and good management practices with some reasonable degree of effectiveness in developing and supervising subordinates, delegation and use of controls, decision making, and communications.

G. Exhibits some reasonable degree of coordinative and cooperative behavior in a positive manner with other college personnel in carrying out the college's mission, institutional goals, and position goals.

IV. *Above Average Performance*

A. Has achieved 85–95 percent of the objectives of his position for the year, as prioritized and agreed upon with his supervisor.

B. Fulfills the key areas of his job description which are normally included under "regular" or "routine" objectives, and fulfills almost all of the duties to meet the total requirements of the position.

C. Produces a quality and quantity of work with a high degree of thoroughness, accuracy, and creativity, exceeding consistently what is required to meet minimum and maximum standards of the position, and within appropriate deadlines.

D. Manages his work area with a high degree of consideration for efficient use of area and institutional resources.

E. Manages his work with a high degree of organization and planning, exceeding consistently what is necessary to meet the minimum and maximum requirements and objectives of the position.

F. Exercises leadership, proper use of authority, and good management practices with a high degree of effectiveness in developing and supervising subordinates, delegation and use of controls, decision making, and communications.

G. Exhibits a high degree of coordinative and cooperative behavior in a positive manner with other college personnel in carrying out the college's mission, institutional goals, and position goals.

V. *Meritorious—Superior*

A. Has achieved 95 percent or above of the objectives of his position for the year, as prioritized and agreed upon with his supervisor.

B. Fulfills the key areas of his job description which are normally included under "regular" or "routine" objectives, and fulfills all of the duties to meet the total requirements of the position.

C. Produces a quality and quantity of work with a very high degree of thoroughness, accuracy, and creativity, exceeding consistently what is required to meet minimum and maximum standards of the position, and within appropriate deadlines.

D. Manages his work area with a very high degree of consideration for efficient use of resources.

E. Manages his work with a very high degree of organization and planning, exceeding consistently what is necessary to meet the minimum and maximum requirements and objectives of the position.

F. Exercises leadership, proper use of authority, and good management practices with a very high degree of effectiveness in developing and supervising subordinates, delegation and use of controls, decision making, and communications.

G. Exhibits a very high degree of coordinative and cooperative behavior in a positive manner with other college personnel in carrying out the college's mission, institutional goals, and position goals.

Implementation Procedures

Date of Interview_____

Performance Appraisal Form

I. NAME_____POSITION_____

Date of Employment_____Time in Position_____

Length of Interview_____

Prior Appraisal Date_____

Time under appraiser's supervision $\overline{\text{Years} \qquad \text{Months}}$

II. REVIEW OF PROGRESS
(Note departures from or adjustments to objectives, etc.)

III. CLIMATE OF INTERVIEW

IV. DEVELOPMENTAL PLAN (List suggested improvements, personal development, suggested activities to be undertaken)

V. COMMENTS

_____

Appraisee's Signature

_____

Supervisor's Signature

_____

Date

Implementation Procedures

V. SUMMARY APPRAISAL

| | Generally satisfactory— | Satisfactory— Normal Expectancy |
| Marginal Unsatisfactory | improvement needed | |

Marginal
Unsatisfactory

Generally
satisfactory—
improvement
needed

Satisfactory—
Normal Expectancy

□ | − | | + | | − | | + |

More than
satisfactory—
above normal
expectancy

Outstanding
and or
exceptional

| − | | + | □

COMMENTS:

147

Proposed Long-Range Planning Decision Matrix

Examples of Alternatives Under Each Charge	1 *Total per Student Cost*	2 *Impact on Student Learning*	3 *Impact on Faculty Attitudes Toward Harper*	4 *Impact on Harper's Service to Community*	5	6	7
A. Area college is to serve							
1. Present area only							
2. Aim for future annexations							
3.							
4.							
5.							
B. Type and number of students served							
1. Accept all new students who apply							
2. Be selective by program							
3. Design policy and program to retain 95% of students who wish to return							
4.							
5.							
6.							
C. Programs and services							
1. Cultural center							
2. Cable TV							
3. Credits by exam							

4. Learning Resources Center serving whole community
5.
6.
7.

D. Curricular changes and instructional strategy innovations
1. Cross divisional teaching
2. Modular scheduling
3. Experimental subdivision
4. Restructured grading system
5.
6.
7.

E. Orderly expansion of physical environment
1. Second campus
2. Central campus and satellites
3. Open 24 hours per day
4.
5.
6.

F. Financial plan
1. Seek local private funding
2. Increase tuition
3. Seek more federal grants
4. Maintain constant cost level
5.
6.
7.

Innovative College Management

Job Description Questionnaire

Date: _____

Incumbent: _____

IMPORTANT: Please read the entire form before making any entries. Think only of the job in answering the questionnaire. It is the job that is being analyzed and not the qualifications of any person. Please answer all questions.

Job Title: _____

Division
or Dept.: _____

Immediate Superior–Title: _____

Name: _____

A. PURPOSE OR FUNCTION OF THE JOB (Why does the job exist?)

B. DESCRIPTION OF DUTIES (List duties in order of their importance. Give the percentage of time you spend on each duty. Be sure to include all periodic and irregular duties.)

C. REQUIREMENTS OF THE JOB:
1. What is the absolute minimum amount of formal education or its equivalent required for this job? State kind and reasons.
2. Given the above amount of education, how much prior experience is needed before coming on the job, state kind, time required and where secured.
3. With the above education and past experience, what new

150

things have to be learned on the job and how much time is normally required to achieve competent performance?

4. Is this person responsible for the supervision and direction of others? How many?
5. What are the difficulties involved in this job:
   a. What decisions must the job-holder make, independent of his supervisor?
   b. How important are the deadlines in this job?
6. What are the responsibilities of this job:
   a. For materials processed, received, handled, stored or sold by the employee or his subordinates?
   b. For contact with the general public? For what purpose?
   c. For cash or negotiable properties?
   d. For accuracy of records and reports?
   e. For confidential information?

RECOMMENDED FOR GRADE LEVEL:

Prepared By: _____
Name and Title

Approved By: _____
Name and Title

Job Evaluation Plan

The ultimate objective of job evaluation is to establish an equitable schedule of wages or salaries. A relationship can be determined between one job and another, ranging from those of minimum difficulty and responsibility to those of maximum difficulty and responsibility. To determine this relative value, it is necessary to make a job-to-job comparison, considering several factors. In order to reduce errors in judgment, each of the factors is subdivided into degrees, with a definition for each degree.

The factors listed below form the basis for evaluation, in that they cover most phases of a job which tend to justify salary differentials.

151

Innovative College Management

	Factors	Degrees and Points					
		1	2	3	4	5	6
1.	Previous Related Experience Required	0	20	40	60	80	100
2.	Education Required	15	30	45	60	75	90
3.	Scope of Duties	10	20	30	45	60	75
4.	Initiative Required	5	10	20	35	50	65
5.	Responsibility for Supervising	5	10	20	35	50	65
6.	Mental Effort Required	5	10	20	30	45	60
7.	Contacts Required	5	10	15	20	30	45
8.	Responsibility for Error	5	10	15	20	30	40
9.	Physical Effort Required	5	10	15	20	25	30
10.	Working Conditions	5	10	15	20	25	30

Please remember that this plan intends to evaluate the job, rather than the person doing the job.

Performance Standards for Boards of Trustees

A performance standard is a written statement or condition that should exist when a job has been properly accomplished.

1. To approve a clearly written statement of the purpose for which the organization exists.
2. To develop written statements of the powers of the board of trustees and the duties and responsibilities interpreted from state statute or charter.
3. To establish college policies consistent with the law as the board may deem best in meeting the purposes of the college.
4. To develop a code of ethics for individual trustee behavior.
5. To develop and approve a contemporary set of by-laws covering such topics as *legal basis and authority, elections, membership* (number and terms, qualifications, geographical distribution, nominations, authority for filling vacancies)

152

Implementation Procedures

organization (annual meeting, officers of the board, term of office, duties of officers, consultants to the board, committee structure if any), *meetings* (regular, special, preparation, order of business, preliminary procedures, authority to conduct business, citizen participation, quorum).

6. To develop and execute, on a regular basis, a plan for evaluating the impact of board policies, as well as for updating the policies.

7. To appoint a president in whom the board has confidence and who will continue to enjoy the support of the board.

8. To define the position of the president in a formal job description.

9. To agree on a general succession plan or a planned approach for filling the president's position.

10. To establish a standard of performance for the president which is agreed to by the board and the president.

11. To call for and approve a specific long-range plan for meeting the objectives of the college.

12. To devise and implement a plan for the regular evaluation of the board of trustees.

13. To call for evaluation systems throughout the organization which identify individual performance and provide appropriate rewards for various performance levels.

14. To agree on the job description for the chairman of the board.

15. To delineate the number and type, the duties and responsibilities, the objectives and performance schedule for each board committee or task force.

16. To set up a system of staff support for individual trustees, particularly the chairman of the board, through the office of the president.

17. To establish a procedure for the identification and acknowledgement of individual board member strengths and weaknesses in order to accomplish a balanced selection process should a vacancy occur on the board of trustees unexpectedly.

18. To design and implement an orientation program for new trustees and a system for evaluating its effectiveness.

19. To prepare and approve a job description for board members.
20. To define and agree upon the distinction between outstanding policy statements and statements of procedure utilized in implementing policy.
21. To carry out with sensitivity the role of representing the institution to its public while at the same time recognizing the need for representing the public to the institution, but in all cases to serve as a timely and appropriate buffer for the institution in time of need.

Board Chairman Job Description

1. To preside at all meetings of the board in an efficient and effective manner and set the general tone for each meeting through positive leadership.
2. To participate jointly with other members of the board in the conduct of appropriate organizational affairs, being careful to mediate and not to dominate the board by virtue of his position.
3. To expedite decision-making and voting of the board after due deliberation and to persuade the board to abide by the majority-rule principle.
4. To appoint board committees in accordance with the by-laws and call for performance reports on a timely basis.
5. To stimulate the board and extract the opinion of each individual where appropriate and to serve as a catalyst for encouraging the members to ask discerning questions.
6. To advise and consult with the president of the college on major problems.
7. To consult with the president on the content and order of the trustee meeting agendas.
8. To establish and maintain, on behalf of the board, good relationships with the press, governmental units, and the public.
9. To carry out special assignments on behalf of the board and to act as spokesman for the board.
10. To channel to the administration requests made by citizens

154

and other board members for special information about the college.

11. To provide leadership and recommend appropriate in-service training, such as attendance at trustee conferences, utilization of outside resource consultants, and planning of special trustee programs.

12. To initiate, on a regular basis, the evaluation of the performance of the board as a whole.

13. To consult with other trustees, on a timely basis, who are not carrying out their agreed-upon responsibilities or who are violating board by-laws, policies, and practices.

14. To serve as a catalyst in initiating evaluation of top executive performance on a regular basis and to lead compensation discussions of the board on behalf of the president.

15. To insure that the board has adequate advance information and sufficient lead time for deliberation of a topic prior to decision-making.

16. To provide leadership in having the board deliberate appropriate topics as opposed to matters which should be delegated or on which the board should receive recommendations from the administration and faculty.

Bibliography

Addison-Wesley Series on Organization Development. Reading, Mass.: Addison-Wesley, 1969.

A five-book series by six authors on the subject of organization development. The authors deal effectively with the nature of organization development, strategies of organization development, process consultation, third party consultation, and developing organizations.

ALBERS, H. H. *Principles of Management.* New York: Wiley, 1969.

A basic managerial publication covering core elements of managerial action—planning, communication, and motivation.

ARGYRIS, C. *Management and Organizational Development.* New York: McGraw-Hill, 1971.

Documentation of actual experiences of three top management groups seeking to develop the full potential of the technical and human resources of their organizations and to unleash their power to grow profitably in both economic and human terms.

BALDRIDGE, V. J. *Academic Governance*. Berkeley, Calif.: McCutchan, 1971.

This publication resulted from a review of the literature on academic governance. The author has collected twenty-six articles resulting from carefully planned social science research projects, classic statements from national study commisions, institution self-evaluations, and union leaders.

BECKHARD, R. *Organization Development: Strategies and Models*. Reading, Mass.: Addison-Wesley, 1969.

This publication, written for managers, training development specialists, and students of management, provides a description of the state of the art of organizational development and offers insight and criteria on which to make decisions and plan and conduct organization development, programs, and activities.

BELCHER, D. W. *Wage and Salary Administration*. Englewood Cliffs, N.J.: Prentice-Hall, 1962.

A useful handbook designed to help every manager make fair and firm decisions in handling wage and salary responsibilities and to ensure their acceptance by employees.

BENNIS, W. G. *Organization Development: Its Nature, Origins, and Prospects*. Reading, Mass.: Addison-Wesley, 1969.

This publication, a primer on organizational development, provides basic information for practicing managers and

Bibliography

students of this educational strategy. Written in clear style, with a minimum of jargon and many excellent examples, the book provides a true contribution to the literature on the subject.

BLAKE, R. R., SHEPARD, H. A., AND MOUTON, J. S. *Managing Intergroup Conflict in Industry.* Houston: Gulf, 1964.

One of the most important managerial skills is the ability to successfully manage and resolve conflicts between groups that work together. In this book the author shows nine possible methods for dealing with conflict, eight of which have side effects detrimental to the accomplishment of organizational objectives and goals.

BOLTON, E. C., AND GENCK, F. "Universities and Management." *Journal of Higher Education,* 1971, *42* (4), 279–291.

Two management consultants provide a perceptive discussion of improvements needed in college and university management. Bolton and Genck suggest universities have been slow to respond to the increased demands for management; they have too few management positions and too few managers. The authors distribute the blame to trustees, the organization structure, and the inappropriate staffing at various levels of the administrative hierarchy.

BORMANN, E. G., HOWELL, W. S., NICHOLS, R. G., AND SHAPIRO, G. L. *Interpersonal Communication in the Modern Organization.* Englewood Cliffs, N.J.: Prentice-Hall, 1969.

The authors of this text share seventy-five years of collective experience analyzing the communication problems of organizations. Each a recognized authority in interpersonal communication, they have had experience in tailoring a training program in communications to meet the needs of a variety of organizations.

BROWN, R. E. *Judgment in Administration*. New York: McGraw-Hill, 1966.

An author's keen insight and perceptive treatment of the practicing judgment of administrators. The book concerns itself more with the failure of administration than with the causes of success by attempting to point out hazards and pitfalls to good judgment.

Carnegie Commission on Higher Education. *The Open-Door Colleges: Policies for Community Colleges*. New York: McGraw-Hill, 1970.

A report with recommendations by the Carnegie Commission on the role of the community college in higher education and proposals of policies for future development.

Carnegie Commission on Higher Education. *The Fourth Revolution: Instructional Technology in Higher Education*. New York: McGraw-Hill, 1972a.

A report with recommendations by the Carnegie Commission suggesting greater use of technology for administrative, research, and instructional activities in higher education.

Carnegie Commission on Higher Education. *The More Effective Use of Resources: An Imperative for Higher Education*. New York: McGraw-Hill, 1972b.

A report with recommendations by the Carnegie Commission on the more effective use of resources toward the accomplishment of institutional goals.

CARR, R. K., AND VAN EYCK, D. K. *Collective Bargaining Comes to the Campus*. Washington, D.C.: American Council on Education, 1973.

Bibliography

A study that examines the development of faculty collective bargaining at four-year colleges and universities since 1969. A valuable addition to the field of public collective bargaining.

CHEIT, E. F. *The New Depression in Higher Education.* New York: McGraw-Hill, 1971.

A study whose purpose was to make available correct, factual analyses of the nature of the financial crisis as it affected selected collegiate institutions of various types throughout the United States.

CRIBBIN, J. J. *Effective Managerial Leadership.* New York: American Management Association, 1972.

A cleverly written response to the requests by managers for realistic grids that can be translated into appropriate managerial behavior during regular work day situations.

DEEGAN, A. *Management by Objectives.* n.d.

This is a workbook, containing descriptive material, reference reading, and worksheets to be used in the implementation of MBO in both profit-making and not-for-profit organizations.

DRUCKER, P. F. *The Practice of Management.* New York: Harper and Row, 1954.

Industrial consultant and research author Peter Drucker provides one of the classic publications in the field of management. His discussion of the knowledge and experience needed for the successful practice of management and his advancement of information for aspiring and practicing managers provide an irreplaceable guide having great impact in the field of management.

Innovative College Management

DRUCKER, P. F. *Managing for Results.* New York: Harper and Row, 1964.

A practical "what to do" rather than theoretical presentation. The author combines specific economic analysis with a discussion of the managerial force required for business prosperity.

DRUCKER, P. F. *The Effective Executive.* New York: Harper and Row, 1966.

The author discusses the attributes of the effective executive and defines this individual as one who gets the right things done. He identifies five habits or practices essential to effectiveness, all of which can be learned.

DRUCKER, P. F. *The Age of Discontinuity.* New York: Harper and Row, 1969.

Peter Drucker perceptively discusses four major changes taking place within our politics, our society, and our economy, noting that the changes are visible but that we scarcely accept the new forms that are creating tomorrow's society.

EURICH, A. C. *Reforming American Education.* New York: Harper and Row, 1969.

A provocative discussion of the call for significant changes in our educational system, a call for innovation and receptivity to constructive change that will result in improving our schools and colleges.

EURICH, A. C. "Plan or Perish." *College and University Journal,* 1970, 9(3), 18–22.

The president of the Academy for Educational Develop-

Bibliography

ment, Inc., cautions colleges to engage in vigorous planning lest someone else provide the planning for them. In reviewing critical problems facing colleges today, the author sets forth persuasive arguments for colleges to initiate sound planning processes to avoid encroachments from the outside.

EWING, D. W. *Long-Range Planning for Management.* New York: Harper and Row, 1972.

The third edition of a popular handbook designed to serve the needs of practitioners, teachers, and students of long-range planning.

FENDROCK, J. J. *Managing in Times of Radical Change.* New York: American Management Association, 1971.

A thoughtful discussion of the need for managers to be more sensitive to the world outside their offices and to be in a position to respond more gracefully to the changing demands of their environment, to the people with whom they work, and to the implementation of new managerial techniques.

FREEMAN, R. A. *Crisis in College Finance?* Washington, D.C.: Institute of Social Science Research, 1965.

An avowed conservative fiscal economist sets forth his views on how best to deal with the crisis in college finance.

GARDNER, J. W. *Excellence: Can We Be Equal and Excellent Too?* New York: Harper and Row, 1961.

An insightful discussion about excellence and the conditions under which excellence is possible in our society as well as of the kinds of equality that can and must be honored.

Innovative College Management

GARDNER, J. W. "How to Prevent Organizational Dry Rot." *Harper's Magazine*, 1965a, 231 (1385), 20–26.

John Gardner presents nine rules of organizational renewal relevant to organizations such as business and industrial companies, governmental agencies, colleges and universities, and banks.

GARDNER, J. W. *Self Renewal.* New York: Harper and Row, 1965b.

John Gardner discusses the great tasks of renewal facing the nation in government, education, race relations, urban development, international affairs, and in the minds and hearts of men.

GARDNER, J. W. *The Recovery of Confidence.* New York: Norton, 1970.

Public servant, scholar, and author John Gardner addresses himself to and presents meaningful insight into some of the most difficult questions facing our nation. What should our goals as a nation be? Can we design a society of continous renewal? What has happened to our confidence as a people? Can we regain it? Why is it so difficult to accomplish social change?

GELLERMAN, S. W. *Management by Motivation.* New York: American Management Association, 1968.

The author stresses the options management has for affecting motivation through administrative action and supports his arguments with behavioral science data.

GOBLE, F. *Excellence in Leadership.* New York: American Management Association, 1972.

Bibliography

A publication reflecting research studies and case histories from business and industry on the topic of leadership and organizational dynamics. The author does a laudable job of describing what leaders are and what they must know and do in directing a successful organization.

GORDON, W. J. J. *Synectics.* New York: Harper and Row, 1961.

This publication is an interim report on the research of the Cambridge Synectics group, whose objective is to develop an operational concept of human creativity and to test the concept. The author describes the evolution of synectics theory, the hypothesis of the theory, and case implementations of the theory.

HANSEN, K. G. (Ed.) *A Classification Plan for Staff Positions at Colleges and Universities.* Urbana, Ill.: College and University Personnel Association, 1968.

A clearly written classification plan for staff positions at colleges and universities. Contains not only a collection of class specifications by areas of work but also includes sections dealing with principles and purposes of a classification plan, the development of such a plan, a related pay plan, position audits, and the maintenance of an effective plan.

HERSEY, P., AND BLANCHARD, K. H. *Management of Organizational Behavior: Utilizing Human Resources.* Englewood Cliffs, N.J.: Prentice-Hall, 1969.

A clear discussion of behavior of people within organizations based on the belief that an organization is a unique living structure whose basic component is the individual. The main concentration is on the interaction of people, motivation, and leadership.

165

HERZBERG, F. *Work and the Nature of Man*. New York: World, 1966.

One of the nation's better known behavioral scientists reveals his theory on work and the nature of man in this third printing publication. This analysis resulted from interchanges between an academic behavioral scientist and business industrial managers throughout the United States and many parts of Europe.

HERZBERG, F. "One More Time: How Do You Motivate Employees?" *Harvard Business Review*, 1968, *46* (1), 53–62.

Herzberg discusses the results of his research in a classic article on his theory of motivating employees within an organization. His discussion of the myths of motivation and job enrichment provide stimulating reading for managers in search of ways to gain increased productivity from employees.

HUGHES, C. L. *Goal Setting*. New York: American Management Association, 1965.

An industrial psychologist explains in meaningful practical language how to recognize the needs for self-fulfillment and job satisfaction, how to stimulate goal-setting behavior in all employees, and how to make management by objectives a reality.

HUMBLE, J. W. *Management by Objectives in Action*. New York: McGraw-Hill, 1970.

Highlights the problem areas and special difficulties encountered in applying management by objectives and shows how they have been overcome.

Bibliography

JENNINGS, E. E. *The Executive in Crisis.* East Lansing: Michigan State University Business Studies, 1965.

An insightful discussion of the nature and causes of executive anxiety.

JENNINGS, E. E. *Executive Success.* New York: Appleton-Century-Crofts, 1967a.

A study of the kinds of stresses that men at the top of organizations have to learn to overcome and master.

JENNINGS, E. E. *The Mobile Manager.* Ann Arbor: Bureau of Industrial Relations, Graduate School of Business Administration, University of Michigan, 1967b.

A study of the mobility patterns of managers and executives that should stimulate more precise methods of executing managerial development and personnel selection.

JURAN, J. M., AND LOUDEN, J. K. *The Corporate Director.* New York: American Management Association, 1966.

Although this text is written in depth about the responsibilities and powers of the corporate director, a dedicated trustee serving other than a corporate organization could well extrapolate ideas which would make him more effective.

KEANE, G. F. "Strengthening College Administration." *Management Controls,* 1970, *17*(3), 56–61.

An insightful article by a senior management consultant relating his views on ways of strengthening college management. Keane suggests clearer goal definition, greater consideration of alternatives, improved information systems, the establishment of intensive training programs for college administrators, an increased supply of manpower for mid-

167

dle-management positions, and improved resource allocation directly related to institutional goals and appropriate priorities.

KEPNER, C. H., AND TREGUE, B. B. *The Rational Manager.* New York: McGraw-Hill, 1965.

A classic text on a systematic approach to improving managerial problem-solving and decision-making. The authors point out and provide guidance for developing a critical managerial skill—asking the right questions at the right time.

KOONTZ, H. *The Board of Directors and Effective Management.* New York: McGraw-Hill, 1967.

An award-winning publication that defines the role of the board of directors in top management in assuring that an organization is well managed.

LAHTI, R. E. "15 Ways to Increase Staff Productivity." *College and University Business,* 1973, *54*(6), 37.

The author presents an addition to the conventional resource model of higher education, which is generally confined to four major categories: tuition, state aid, miscellaneous, and taxes. He maintains that increased staff productivity is another resource to which attention must be paid and goes on to discuss fifteen ways of expanding personnel productivity.

LESSINGER, L. "It's Time for 'Accountability' in Education." *Nation's Business,* August 1971, 54–56.

Lessinger, a man of distinguished administrative service in public schools and government, sets forth a frank discussion of the inability of public education to effectively measure

Bibliography

its output. His charge that schools would be unable to deliver if the public demanded better performance is backed up by provocative suggestions on how schools can become more accountable.

LIKERT, R. *New Patterns of Management.* New York: McGraw-Hill, 1961.

A volume written especially for individuals actively engaged in management and supervision and for students of administration and organization. A triple-award-winning book recognized for advancing the position of management within institutions.

LIKERT, R. *The Human Organization.* New York: McGraw-Hill, 1967.

A book describing a new system of management that has potential for achieving better productivity, above average financial success, and improved labor relations. The system discussed evolved from twenty years of active research.

LIPPIT, G. L. *Organizational Renewal.* New York: Meredithy, 1969.

A discussion of research, experiences, and challenges centering around the practitioner and the student of organization life. The author discusses the challenge to all organizations for maintaining relevancy to the age in which they live.

LIVINGSTON, J. S. "Myth of the Well-Educated Manager." *Harvard Business Review,* 1971, *41*(1), 79–89.

Livingston has actively managed hundreds of MBA graduates in his distinguished career as a manager, entrepreneur, and teacher. His hard-hitting discussion of the inability of formal management education programs within universities and industry to develop the traits, knowledge, and skills essential to career success and leadership in a business organization provides provocative reading for executives and management training personnel.

LOEN, R. O. *Manage More by Doing Less.* New York: McGraw-Hill, 1971.

A clear and simple discussion of the difference between managing and nonmanaging activities on the job.

LOPEZ, F. M., JR. *Personnel Interviewing.* New York: McGraw-Hill, 1965.

A practical book offering detailed guidance on the use of the personnel interview as a specific managerial tool to facilitate effective selection, placement, and motivation of employees.

LOPEZ, F. M., JR. *Evaluating Employee Performance.* Chicago: Public Personnel Association, 1968.

An extensive discussion on the subject of employee performance evaluation.

LOUDEN, J. K. *Making It Happen.* New York: American Management Association, 1971.

A descriptive discourse on ways of accomplishing total involvement resulting in total commitment. The author concentrates on the importance of developing the greatest individual potential and the involvement of the total team in the management processes of organization.

MC BEATH, G., AND RANDS, D. N. *Salary Administration.* (2nd ed.) London: Business Books, 1969.

Bibliography

A revised edition intended to be a practical guide to salary administration practice and philosophy.

MC FEELY, W. M. *Organization Change, Perceptions and Realities.* New York: Conference Board, 1972.

A Conference Board report compiled as a result of in-depth interviews with executives at different levels in fifteen companies of different sizes that have experienced major organization change.

MC GREGOR, D. M. *The Human Side of Enterprise.* New York: McGraw-Hill, 1960.

A perceptive discussion of assumptions about the way to manage people in an organization. Theory X and Theory Y management, as applied to people, are discussed in detail.

MAC KENZIE, R. A. *Managing Time at the Top.* New York: President's Association, American Management Association, 1970.

A research study that focuses on the effective utilization of time of top managers.

MALI, P. *Managing by Objectives.* New York: Wiley, 1972.

A positive operating guide that introduces a systems approach for installing, developing, and operating a management by objectives system.

MANN, A. J. *The Failure of Success.* New York: Amacom, American Management Association, 1972.

A series of case studies from leading organizations collected to provide empirical evidence on the use of new managerial methods to improve and narrow the gap between an organization's potential and its performance.

Innovative College Management

MARVIN, P. *Management Goals: Guidelines and Accountability.* Homewood, Ill.: Dow Jones-Irwin, 1968.

A thoughtful discussion based on firsthand experience of how men and managers can work together in developing a step by step performance achievement plan.

MASLOW, A. H. *Eupsychian Management.* Homewood, Ill.: Irwin, 1965.

A behavioral scientist's insight into industrial and managerial psychology: the result of a summer visit to an industrial plant for the purpose of studying the interrelations between psychological theory and enlightened modern management.

MITCHELL, W. N. *The Business Executive in a Changing World.* New York: American Management Association, 1965.

From a wide background of knowledge gained through working with many major business organizations, the author analyzes the true role of the executive, the source and use of his power, the factors that motivate his performance, and the steps he must take to increase his own and his company's success.

MYERS, M. S. *Every Employee a Manager.* New York: McGraw-Hill, 1970.

An excellent publication written by an experienced industrial psychologist who summarizes modern behavioral theories and the conditions necessary to make people responsive and creative on the job.

National Industrial Conference Board. *Behavioral Science Concepts and Management Application.* Studies in Personnel

Bibliography

Policy Research Report 216. New York: Conference Board, 1970.

This report examines behavioral science concepts as they evolve from theory to laboratory experiments, to developmental research, and finally to on-the-job applications in managing human resources.

ODIORNE, G. *Management by Objectives.* New York: Pitman, 1965.

A descriptive text of management by objectives. Step by step the author shows how managers jointly identify organization goals and each manager's major responsibilities in terms of results expected of him.

ODIORNE, G. *Management Decisions by Objectives.* Englewood Cliffs, N.J.: Prentice-Hall, 1969.

A comprehensive guide to making successful management decisions as a result of understanding the logic and psychology of the decision-making process.

ODIORNE, G. "Up the Pyramid . . .er Doughnut . . .er Beehive." *Nation's Business,* January 1972, 62–64.

Odiorne, a well-known authority on management, provides a stimulating discussion of corporate organizational models —matrix, bottom-up, collegial, ladder, beehive, project management, task force, and doughnut. His summarizing advice, however, is for organizational executives to get their objectives clear and organize the way that is most likely to help achieve them.

Papers on Efficiency in the Management of Higher Education. Berkeley, Calif.: Carnegic Commission on Higher Education, 1972.

173

Four reports completed as part of an extensive study to explore radical strategies for bringing about considerable improvement in higher education.

RANDALL, C. B. *The Executive in Transition.* New York: McGraw-Hill, 1967.

An experienced executive shares his views on learning to manage. His claim that experience is the best teacher is reinforced by the assessment of his own shortcomings and satisfactions for the benefit of others stumbling up the ladder of responsibility.

REDDIN, W. J. *Managerial Effectiveness.* New York: McGraw-Hill, 1970.

The aim of this text is to make managers and the organizations in which they work more effective by suggesting a value analysis of the individual and offering direct advice on how to improve individual effectiveness.

REDDIN, W. J. *Effective Management by Objectives: The 3-D Method of MBO.* New York: McGraw-Hill, 1971.

A specific application of the 3-D method and the concepts of effectiveness and team implementation utilized in introducing management by objectives. The book is behavorial science in practice.

ROCK, M. L. *Handbook of Wage and Salary Administration.* New York: McGraw-Hill, 1972.

An authoritative handbook of wage and salary administration by a practicing wage and salary consultant who explains how to set up and maintain an effective wage and salary program for the lowest paid hourly worker to the president.

Bibliography

RUSH, H. M. F. *Behavioral Science Concepts and Management Application.* New York: Conference Board, 1970.

A brief exposition of the characteristics or the current state of the art of behavioral science and of its relevance to modern business organizations, followed by a capsule review of the theories and contributions of five of the most influential behavioral scientists.

STEINER, G. A. *The Creative Organization.* Chicago: University of Chicago Press, 1965.

A clear, concise report resulting from a University of Chicago seminar convened for the purpose of identifying and fostering individual and organizational creativity.

TOSI, H. L., RIZZO, J. R., AND CARROLL, S. J. "Setting Goals in Management by Objectives." *California Management Review,* 1970 *12*(4), 70–78.

Three university professors provide a meaningful discussion of important factors to consider in the goal setting process of MBO. Sharing their research and experience in dealing with MBO, they provide excellent pointers and cautions for top and middle management to consider during the implementation of the system.

VALENTINE, R. F. *Performance Objectives for Managers.* New York: American Management Association, 1966.

A clear explanation of a qualitative approach that deals with actual results rather than traditional behavior ratings. The author describes how the concept of managing by objectives can enhance managerial efficiency.

WIKSTROM, W. S. *Managing by—and with—Objectives.* Personnel Policy Study 212. New York: Conference Board, 1968.

Innovative College Management

A research report published by the National Industrial Conference Board that deals with the concept of management by objectives and the practices followed by companies during the implementation of the system.

ZOLLITSCH, H. G., AND LANGSNER, A. *Wage and Salary Administration.* (2nd ed.) Cincinnati: South-Western, 1970.

The revised edition of this text incorporates the most recent compensation principles and the many suggestions of the readers and users of the first edition. The text is aimed at undergraduate and graduate students of wage and salary administration as well as practitioners in industrial engineering and wage and salary administration.

Suggested Periodicals

College and University Business. Chicago: McGraw-Hill.

College Management. Greenwich, Conn.: McMillan Professional Magazines.

The Conference Board Record. New York: Conference Board.

Dun's Review. New York: Dun and Bradstreet.

Fortune. Chicago: Time.

Harvard Business Review. Uxbridge, Mass.: Harvard Business Review.

Journal of College and University Personnel. Washington, D.C.: College and University Personnel Association.

Journal of Higher Education. Columbus: Ohio State University Press.

Bibliography

Management Review. New York: Amacom, American Management Association.

Nation's Business. Washington, D.C.: Nation's Business.

Training and Development Journal. Madison, Wis.: American Society of Training and Development.

Official monthly publication of the American Society of Training and Development, which features most current writings by knowledgeable training and development personalities.

Index

Index

ership, survey on trustees by, 27

Communication, in MBO, 56, 75

Community colleges: challenges to, 115–116; MBO in, 53–65; management development program for, 36–39; priorities of, 7–13; problems facing, 3–6

Compensation: administration of program for, 102–111; characteristics of program for, 105–106; development of program for, 106–107; of exempt employees, 106–108; of faculty, 102–103, 110; goals of program for, 104–105; as management problem, 47–48; trustees related to, 4–5

Conflict resolution, 14, 43–44

Creativity: as MBO characteristic, 56, 74; role of in management, 15–16, 45

D

Decision-making, as managerial skill, 43

DEEGAN, A., 55, 161

Delegation: in MBO, 74–75; as managerial skill, 40

DRUCKER, P. F., 4, 55, 93, 161–162

E

EURICH, A. C., 2–3, 162–163

Evaluation, of MBO, 123–139. *See also* Appraisal

EWING, D. W., 93, 163

G

GARDNER, J. W., 23, 82, 83–84, 163–164

GENCK, F., 103–104, 159

Goals: individual needs related to, 14; institutional, in MBO, 59–60, 63–64; and leadership, 18; setting of, 13–14

GOBLE, F., 164–165

GORDON, W. J. J., 45, 165

Governance, reform needed in, 2–3

H

HERZBERG, F., 6, 166

Higher education, confidence in, 1–2

I

Identity, institutional, and goals, 15

Individuals: involvement of in organization, 16–17, 18; needs of, related to institutional goals, 14

Institutional research: and long-range planning contrasted, 10–11; as managerial skill, 45–46

Involvement, as MBO characteristic, 73–74

J

Job description: in MBO, 61–62, 64; questionnaire for, 150–151; for trustee chairman, 154–155

Job evaluation, form for, 151–152

Job performance, in objective-setting, 69

K

KEANE, G. F., 3, 167–168

180

Index